CLAIM
YOUR
VICTORY
TODAY

CLAIM YOUR VICTORY TODAY

10 Steps That Will Revolutionize Your Life

DR CREFLO A. DOLLAR

FaithWords

NEW YORK   BOSTON   NASHVILLE

FaithWords
Hachette Book Group USA
237 Park Avenue
New York, NY 10017

Visit our Web site at www.faithwords.com.

Printed in the United States of America

Originally published in hardcover by Hachette Book Group USA.

First Trade Edition: October 2007
10 9 8 7 6 5 4 3 2 1

FaithWords is a division of Hachette Book Group USA, Inc.
The FaithWords name and logo is a trademark of
Hachette Book Group USA, Inc.

The Library of Congress has cataloged the hardcover edition as follows:
Dollar, Dr. Creflo A.
Claim your victory today : 10 steps that will revolutionize
your life / by Dr. Creflo A. Dollar.—1st ed.
p. cm.
Summary: "Reveals ten insightful, practical, Bible-based steps
for achieving victory over any problem you may ever
face"—Provided by the publisher.
ISBN-13: 978-0-446-58005-2
ISBN-10: 0-446-58005-8
1. Problem solving—Religious aspects—Christianity.
2. Success—Religious aspects—Christianity.   I. Title
BV4599.5.P75D65   2006
248.4—dc22   2006007545

ISBN 978-0-446-17817-4 (pbk.)

*In the early days of my ministry, God placed
two individuals in my life who impacted me eternally.
Bishop C. L. Carter, Sr., and Minister Laura M. Carter provided
spiritual oversight to me as my pastors and as my teachers.
They cared for me like a son.
Their Christ-like examples, wise counsel, and
faithful prayers made all the difference in how
God set me on His divine course for my life.*

*I dedicate this book to them for their hearts of love
and compassion pertaining to the gift of God they saw in me.
With all my heart, I bless them with my enduring love—always.*

Contents

CLAIM
YOUR
VICTORY
TODAY

Before We Begin:
Is Your Faith Out of Order?

Let all things be done decently and in order.
—1 Corinthians 14:40

∽૭∽ Frustration. I see it on the faces of many believers who tell me they just can't seem to get "this faith stuff" to work for them.

I can sympathize. Early in my Christian life, I too spent a lot of time scratching my head and wondering why I wasn't seeing the miracles I needed so desperately. Now I know that the key to seeing miracle-working power operate consistently in our lives lies in understanding the divine order of faith.

When I talk about "divine order," I'm referring to the fact that God has ordained everything in heaven and on earth to operate according to a predetermined sequence or order. This is especially true where spiritual things are concerned. God's heavenly Kingdom is a place of order.

For example, under the Old Covenant system, the high priest followed a very strict, very detailed sequence of actions before he dared to enter the Holy of Holies. He didn't go waltzing into the Most Holy Place anytime he pleased. I assure you, he would have done so only once. Such a cavalier attitude toward God's prescribed order would have cost him his life. There was a process that had to take place before the high priest could operate in certain aspects of his calling.

The same is true for you and me where faith is concerned. We will never see the miracles and promises of God that will move us from the problem to the solution until we come to understand the divine order of faith.

FOLLOW THE PROCEDURE

Even in everyday life, there is an established order to follow in much of what we do. As the pastor of a large and growing congregation, I frequently run into people who fail to follow the set order. From time to time, for example, an irate church member will come up to me and say, "Pastor, I've been trying to get in to see you for five months!"

I respond by asking how he or she has gone about trying to see me.

"Well, I've dropped by your office several times, and you're either gone or busy or you have someone in your office."

Immediately the problem is evident. There is a simple and well-established procedure in our church for arranging to see the pastor. It is spelled out clearly in our new member orientation. Anyone who wants to see me merely needs to call my secretary, set up an appointment, and show up on the day and time set. That's all there is to it.

I have established a clear order for arranging my office schedule. If you don't follow the order, you probably won't get in to see me. The same is true in the Kingdom of God. The Lord has a set order for everything. First Corinthians 14 makes that very clear:

> For God is not the author of confusion, but of peace, as in all churches of the saints. . . . Let all things be done decently and in order.
>
> —*1 Corinthians 14:33, 40*

NO ORDER, NO MIRACLES

When you neglect God's divine order, His blessings don't flow. Divine order is a prerequisite for miracles and blessings. This truth is illustrated vividly in Jesus' feeding of the five thousand. Before the people could be miraculously blessed, they had to get in order.

❊ *When you neglect God's divine order, His blessings don't flow.*

> For they were about five thousand men. And he said to his disciples, Make them sit down by fifties in a company.
>
> —*Luke 9:14*

Can you imagine the chaos that would have ensued if the disciples had started randomly handing out food to that hungry mob? There would have been a riot!

There's no getting around it. Follow God's set order and you'll get the desired results. Ignore it and you'll end up frustrated and defeated.

So does God have an established order when it comes to overcoming problems? Yes. The Scriptures give us a clear pattern for moving from any problem—be it sickness, debt, lack, family strife, or anything else—to the solution. These steps will work for anyone at any time, regardless of how overwhelming the circumstances are, because these steps represent God's divine order of faith.

Over the years, there has been a lot of good teaching on faith. But I've heard very little on God's prescribed order for using it. I believe that's why we have so many so-called faith failures and so many frustrated Christians. Most don't even know there is a divine order of faith, much less understand what it is.

In the following pages we'll see that God's Word lays out a simple ten-step order for getting from any problem to a miraculous solution. It doesn't matter if you've been a Christian for fifty years or if you were born again five minutes ago. If you will submit yourself to this order, your faith will produce. God's Word guarantees it.

> ❊ *If you will submit yourself to this order, your faith will produce. God's Word guarantees it.*

Before you can submit to God's divine order for faith, however, you need to have a good working understanding of what faith is.

YOU GOTTA HAVE FAITH

The just shall live by faith.

—*Romans 1:17*

Child of God, the time for playing church is over. The King of kings and the Lord of lords is on His way back. And the key to surviving and even thriving in this unprecedented era is knowing how to operate in faith.

We are living in extraordinary times. Signs all around us shout the fact that we are living in the final days of history. In this critical hour, knowing how to operate in faith can literally mean the difference between life and death.

> ❋ *Knowing how to operate in faith can literally mean the difference between life and death.*

That's why it is vital for you to start developing your faith now. If you wait until a crisis is upon you to start learning how to live by faith, you'll be in big trouble. Those who put it off until the last minute will find that it's too late.

NO AVOIDING TROUBLE

Regardless of the time in history in which you're living, if you're a believer one thing is certain: you're going to have trouble. It's not only likely—it's guaranteed. In John 16:33, Jesus says:

These things I have spoken unto you, that in me ye might have peace. In the world ye shall have tribulation: but be of good cheer; I have overcome the world.

It shouldn't come as any great shock when, as a believer, you experience tribulation or trouble. Jesus said it would happen. But praise God, that's not all He said. He also admonished us, "Cheer up! I have overcome the world!"

The world really hasn't changed very much since Jesus' day. Sure, technology has advanced, but human nature is as mean and nasty as ever. Without Jesus, this world is a hostile place. And even with Jesus, we still face trials and tribulation.

The good news is that Jesus tells us to be of good cheer because He has overcome. That knowledge, however, really doesn't help much unless we also understand how He overcame so we can do the same. We need to know what it takes to overcome poverty and lack, what we can do to overcome certain destructive habits, and what is needed to enable us to overcome sickness.

In 1 John 5:4, Jesus offers the answer to our questions:

For whatsoever is born of God overcometh the world: and this is the victory that overcometh the world, even our faith.

There it is. The first prerequisite for overcoming the world is being "born of God." There's no use even trying to be a world overcomer if you're not born again. Then the second part of that verse tells us what enables us to overcome—our faith. Jesus overcame the world by using His faith, and we'll overcome the world using the measure of faith God has given us.

Faith is the key. It hasn't passed away. It's not something out of a dusty old sermon. Faith is fresh, alive, powerful, and as relevant today as at any time in history. If you're going to overcome the world rather than be overcome by it, you're going to do it with your faith.

❋ If you're going to overcome the world rather than be overcome by it, you're going to do it with your faith.

Too many people in the church today are trying to overcome their problems with pop psychology, government programs, or something they read in a magazine somewhere. The truth is, you can't separate victory from faith. To experience victory you have to have faith in God and His Word.

LIVE IT

God is serious about His people's commitment to operating in faith. In fact, four separate times in Scripture, He declares, "The just shall live by faith" (Habbakuk 2:4; Romans 1:17; Galatians 3:11; Hebrews 10:38). Now the Bible says, "In the mouth of two or three witnesses every word may be established" (Matthew 18:16; see also 2 Corinthians 13:1), and here is the testimony of four voices proclaiming the same thing. Do you get the impression God wants us to live by faith?

If you're saved, you're one of the "just." When Jesus washes your sins away you are declared righteous by God Himself. And as one of the just, you must learn to live by faith.

You may say, "I tried that faith thing and it didn't work."

Well, the Bible doesn't say, "The just shall try it out." It says, "The just shall live by faith." You don't dabble in faith. You live it.

❁ *You don't dabble in faith. You live it.*

SO WHAT IS FAITH?

Once you understand that trouble is inevitable and faith is the only thing that will overcome that trouble, the next step is to discover once and for all what this thing called *faith* really is. You may be thinking, *Everybody knows what faith is. It means belief or trust in God and His Word.* Of course, that's part of it. But real faith involves so much more than that, and any biblical discussion of the nature of faith has to start with Hebrews, chapter 11:

Now faith is the substance of things hoped for, the evidence of things not seen. For by it the elders obtained a good report. Through faith we understand that the worlds were framed by the word of God, so that things which are seen were not made of things which do appear. By faith Abel offered unto God a more excellent sacrifice than Cain, by which he obtained witness that he was righteous, God testifying of his gifts: and by it he being dead yet speaketh. By faith Enoch was translated that he should not see death; and was not found, because God had translated him: for before his translation he had this testimony, that he pleased God. But without faith it is impossible to please him: for he that cometh to God must believe that he is, and that he is a rewarder of them that diligently seek him.

—*Hebrews 11:1–6*

Notice the first three words of the first verse: "Now faith *is.*" The first thing you need to understand is that faith operates in the realm of the now. God is not yesterday. God is not tomorrow. God abides in the eternal now. He didn't tell Moses His name was "I WAS." He called Himself "I AM." That's good news, because when you're sick God says, "I AM your healer." When you need finances, He says, "I AM your provider." And when you're in trouble, you don't need deliverance someday—you need it now, and "I AM" is present to deliver.

The next remarkable thing these verses teach us about faith is that it is a substance. "Faith is the substance of things hoped for." In other words, faith is a literal, unseen material. It is "stuff." Verse 3 tells us that faith is the agency through which the physical universe was made:

Through faith we understand that the worlds were framed by the word of God, so that things which are seen were not made of things which do appear.

—*Hebrews 11:3*

Think of it. Everything you see around you is the product of faith-filled words. Think of God's words as spiritual seeds—seeds that have the ability to produce physical things like trees, planets, or money. That's why the Bible is such an enormously powerful thing. From cover to cover, it contains God's faith-filled words, specifically empowered to produce whatever you need in your life.

When you pick up your Bible, you hold in your hands the seeds to produce finances, healing, salvation of your loved ones, a sound mind, restoration of your marriage, or anything else you could possibly need. The tragic fact is that many believers are simply too lazy to pick up their Bible, get the seed out, and plant it. Far too many of us want to just line up in a prayer line, have a minister lay hands on us, and instantaneously—without any effort on our part—see all our problems solved. But it doesn't work that way.

Successful farming takes effort and hard work. A farmer's seed does him no good as long as it lies dormant in the sack. But when he plants his seed, he gets a harvest. Likewise, the seeds of provision in God's Word will never produce for you as long as your Bible gathers dust on your shelf.

> ✻ *The seeds of provision in God's Word will never produce for you as long as your Bible gathers dust on your shelf.*

"But what if I don't know how to plant the seed of God's Word?" That's what this book is all about. As I said in the opening chapter, there is a specific divine order for getting from the problem to the answer. In the next chapter, we will begin with Step 1 on the road to victory.

⌒ Think about It ⌒

1. What is "divine order"?

2. How did the Old Covenant high priest demonstrate divine order?

3. Read and study 1 Corinthians 14:27–33. What happens when God's divine order is ignored?

4. Read Luke 11:1–4. What do you notice about the order of Jesus' prayer? Why is it significant?

5. Have you experienced "faith failures" in your life? If so, identify any that may have occurred because you were ignorant of God's divine order.

6. As a believer, how can you avoid trouble?

7. What are the two keys given in 1 John 5:4 for overcoming the world?

8. How have you tried to overcome your own lack, sickness, or sin?

9. If you are "the just," how does the Bible command you to live? How does a human being qualify to be "the just"?

10. When does faith operate? How do you know?

11. Explain how God created all things. Of what substance do all things consist?

12. Why is your Bible your most valuable possession? What does it contain that you must have to overcome the world?

℘ Reflect on It ℘

For God is not the author of confusion, but of peace, as in all churches of the saints.

—*1 Corinthians 14:33*

Let all things be done decently and in order.

—*1 Corinthians 14:40*

My prayer in the power of the Word:

_____

_____

_____

_____

_____

I have told you these things, so that in Me you may have [perfect] peace and confidence. In the world you have tribulation and trials and distress and frustration; but be of good cheer [take courage; be confident, certain, undaunted]! For I have overcome the world. [I have deprived it of power to harm you and have conquered it for you.]

—*John 16:33* AMP

My prayer in the power of the Word:

_____

_____

_____

_____

_____

Now faith is the assurance (the confirmation, the title deed) of the things [we] hope for, being the proof of things [we] do not see and the conviction of their reality [faith perceiving as real fact what is not revealed to the senses]. For by [faith—trust and holy fervor born of faith] the men of old had divine testimony borne to them and obtained a good report. By faith we understand that the worlds [during the successive ages] were framed (fashioned, put in order, and equipped for their intended purpose) by the word of God, so that what we see was not made out of things which are visible.

—Hebrews 11:1–3 AMP

My prayer in the power of the Word:

_____

_____

_____

_____

_____

_____

Do It

1. Get out your calendar, daily planner, or PDA. Set aside at least thirty minutes, several times a week, to focus on revolutionizing your walk with God through mastering the ten steps set forth in this book. Write it down, schedule it in, and resolve to stick to it!

2. Plan a location for your daily study, whether it's in your home, your office, the local park, or a combination. Make sure it's a quiet place where you won't be interrupted.

3. Prepare your materials. Look around your house for an unused notebook or spiral binder, or go down to the supermarket and purchase an inexpensive journal. Gather a couple of your favorite pens, your Bible, and this book. Place everything where you'll use them each day, or in a backpack or bag for easy access when you're on the go.

4. Talk to your family members and friends. Explain your new daily commitment and ask for their support and prayers as you embark on this journey.

Pray for God's leading and wisdom as you delve into the ten steps to victory!

Step One:
Identify the Problem

In the world ye shall have tribulation: but be
of good cheer; I have overcome the world.

—*John 16:33*

Before you can expect to get from the problem to the answer, you must first clearly define and understand the exact nature of the problem you are facing. Is it spiritual? Physical? Financial? Emotional? Whatever it is, the first step in conquering it is facing it head-on and identifying what it truly is.

That may seem like a pretty obvious place to start, but you'd be surprised how many believers think that being born again means experiencing no more problems. Then, when they are faced with an attack or an affliction, they don't know how to pinpoint it or what to do.

Make no mistake about it—problems are going to come. As we saw previously in John 16:33, Jesus said we could bank on it. He said, "In the world ye shall have tribulation."

In Philippians 3:10, Paul shed additional light on the issue:

That I may know him [Christ], and the power of his resurrection, and the fellowship of his sufferings, being made conformable unto his death.

What does it mean to know the fellowship of Jesus' sufferings? Probably not what you think. This verse isn't telling you to be prepared to live in ongoing pain and suffering. Jesus was an overcomer. He obtained absolute victory in every trial, temptation, and test He faced. Therefore, when you enter into the fellowship of His sufferings, you don't have to just gracefully surrender to them: you can take anything the Devil throws at you and toss it right back in his face. And how do you do that?

There is only one way you are going to truly be a partaker in Jesus' victory, and that's through the Word of God. The seeds of victory over any circumstance you may ever face are in your Bible right now. But be prepared. The Devil doesn't take kindly to your digging into the source of his defeat.

> ❂ *The seeds of victory over any circumstance you may ever face are in your Bible right now.*

SATAN THE STEALER

One of the first things you'll notice when you start getting serious about planting God's Word in your heart and mind is an increase in problems. That surprises a lot of believers.

"But I thought diving into the Bible was going to quickly solve all my problems!" If that's what you think, child of God, you're mistaken. The Word doesn't erase all problems from your life, but it does give you the power to overcome any problem. And as we learn from Jesus in the parable of the sower, Satan's number-one objective is to steal that Word from your heart. If he can't do that, he'll use problems to try to choke it out:

The sower soweth the word. And these are they by the way side, where the word is sown; but when they have heard, Satan cometh immediately, and taketh away the word that was sown in their hearts. And these are they likewise which are sown on stony ground; who, when they have heard the word, immediately receive it with gladness; and have no root in themselves, and so endure but for a time: afterward, when affliction or persecution ariseth for the word's sake, immediately they are offended.

—*Mark 4:14–17*

Notice that first sentence: "The sower soweth the word." We saw in the introduction that the Bible contains seeds of answers for every problem you face.

Jesus said, "And these are they by the way side, where the word is sown; but when they have heard. . . ." Hearing the Word is vitally important. If Satan can stop you from hearing the Word concerning a certain subject, he's on his way to defeating you in that area of your life.

"But when they have heard, Satan cometh immediately, and taketh away the word that was sown in their hearts." Who comes? Satan. When does he come? Immediately.

As long as you ignore God's Word, you're no threat to Satan. But when you start planting God's Word in your heart, he flies into action. He simply can't permit you to put the awesome, creative forces of faith-filled words to work in your life. It will undo everything he has been working for where you're concerned.

> ❈ *As long as you ignore God's Word,*
> *you're no threat to Satan.*

If he fails to steal the Word from your heart as soon as you receive it, the Devil's next ploy will be to come at you with trouble and cause you to be offended at God. Remember Jesus' parable: "When they have heard the word, immediately receive it with gladness; and have no root in themselves, and so endure but for a time: afterward, when affliction or persecution ariseth for the word's sake, immediately they are offended."

This represents one of the two main sources of problems in any believer's life. Trials, persecution, affliction, and trouble all can come as Satan desperately tries to keep God's Word from doing its work in your heart.

SELF-INFLICTED WOUNDS

We've seen how problems can come as Satan tries to choke out the seed of the Word in your life. The other way trouble can enter is through the bad seeds you plant yourself. Look at 1 Peter 2:20:

> For what glory is it, if, when ye be buffeted for your faults, ye shall take it patiently?

And 1 Peter 4:15:

> But let none of you suffer as a murderer, or as a thief, or as an evildoer, or as a busybody in other men's matters.

These verses tell us many Christians suffer not because of an attack of the Devil but because of their own actions. Sins, evil words, and unrighteous attitudes can all result in an increase in trouble.

I recall hearing about a young lady who complained about constantly being approached by rude and offensive men. She prayed and spoke the Word and wondered why she wasn't seeing any results. Then someone pointed out that she tended to wear dresses that looked like they were painted on. She dressed like a loose woman and was shocked when men treated her like one. In reality, she was simply reaping a harvest of bad seeds she had sown.

BE A JUDGE

The first step in God's divine order of faith is identifying the source and nature of the problem you are facing. That requires you to become a good judge. Be honest with yourself and with God, and determine the exact source of the problem. Have you caused the problem or are you under attack? If it is a result of past sins or mistakes, repent and make appropriate restitution. If you are under attack, work to gain a specific understanding of the root. Is it sickness, fear, family strife, financial lack, or something else? Once you know precisely what your problem is and where it's coming from, you're ready to take the next step in God's divine order of faith.

The first step in God's divine order of faith is identifying the source and nature of the problem you are facing.

❧ Think about It ❧

1. What is the first thing you should do when you have a problem?

2. Read James 1:2–3. Why should we "count it all joy" when we have troubles?

3. Read Philippians 3:10. Does this mean you are to give in to suffering and bear it with a smile?

4. Where are your seeds of victory for every problem, trial, and tribulation?

5. When you start putting God's Word in your heart, what happens?

6. Read the parable of the sower in Mark, chapter 4. What are some ways the Word can be stolen from you?

7. Can you think of a time when your faith was shaken by a negative turn of events in your life? Were you angry with God? How did you handle it?

8. Read 1 Peter 2:20 and 4:15. How do we cause suffering in our own lives?

9. Read Psalm 13. At what point did David turn from despair to hope? What do you think caused this switch?

10. What is one of the greatest advantages of going through the process of identifying our problems?

11. What is the first step in God's divine order of faith? What does this require of you?

12. What questions do you need to ask yourself in order to be a good judge of what's happening in your life? What if you are having trouble seeing the truth?

⟋ Reflect on It ⟍

My brethren, count it all joy when ye fall into divers temptations; knowing this, that the trying of your faith worketh patience. But let patience have her perfect work, that ye may be perfect and entire, wanting nothing. If any of you lack wisdom, let him ask of God, that giveth to all men liberally, and upbraideth not; and it shall be given him.

—*James 1:2–5*

My prayer in the power of the Word:

_____

_____

_____

_____

_____

The sower soweth the word. And these are they by the way side, where the word is sown; but when they have heard, Satan cometh immediately, and taketh away the word that was sown in their hearts. And these are they likewise which are sown on stony ground; who, when they have heard the word, immediately receive it with gladness; and have no root in themselves, and so endure but for a time: afterward, when affliction or persecution ariseth for the word's sake, immediately they are offended.

—*Mark 4:14–17*

My prayer in the power of the Word:

_____

_____

_____

_____

_____

Search me, O God, and know my heart: try me, and know my thoughts.

—*Psalm 139:23*

My prayer in the power of the Word:

_____

_____

_____

_____

_____

Do It

1. Study the parable of the sower (Mark 4:14–17) and this chapter's description of how Satan attempts to keep us from hearing or absorbing the Word. In your journal, make a list of all the ways that Satan tries to steal the Word from you. Think about how he keeps you from hearing it in the first place, the ways he prevents it from permeating your heart, and how he causes you to be offended at God, thus negating the power of the Word. Now jot down some ideas for defeating Satan in his tactics. Make a commitment to carry out some of these plans this week.

2. Write one sentence that describes the problem(s) that brought you to this book in the first place. Below that sentence, make a list of everything you can think of that contributes to the problem or that led you to where you are today. See if this helps you delve beneath the surface and identify the root issue.

3. If you feel comfortable sharing your situation with a trusted friend or advisor, contact the person and make an appointment to talk by phone or to meet in person. When you meet, let your friend know that you are embarking on Step 1 of this journey and would like his help in understanding and identifying the troubles you hope to overcome. Go into the conversation with honesty and

openness, and listen carefully to your friend's assessment. Afterward, note any insights in your journal.

4. Determine whether you need to make restitution to someone before continuing on this journey. If so, carefully consider how best to go about it. Discuss it with your pastor if necessary. Make a plan, including the date, time, and place, to carry out your restitution. Then follow through.

5. Read psalms that speak of troubles and trials. (You may want to look at Psalms 3, 6, 9, 10, 15, 22, 35, 39, 42, 43, 88, 102.) Notice how the writers express themselves fully and honestly, not holding back their emotions. Pay attention to how they talk to God about the details of their afflictions, and how they articulate their distress. Observe the transition from complaint to praise. Now write your own psalm in your journal. Write in normal, everyday language, expressing to God your suffering, your anguish, your worry, your guilt, or your grief. See if there is a point at which your psalm naturally evolves from focusing on your problem to expressing hope and worship. Repeat this exercise until you can articulate the exact nature of your problem.

6. Finally, write down a clear and concise statement of the problems you need to overcome, and make a list of any Scriptures that might help you in your journey.

Step Two:
Make a Quality Decision

Multitudes, multitudes in the valley of decision:
for the day of the LORD is near in the valley of
decision.

—*Joel 3:14*

Once you have a handle on what the problem is, the
next step is to make a quality decision to overcome it by faith. In
other words, you must choose.

The ability to choose, our free moral agency, is one of the
main ways in which we're made in the image of God. Every person born into the earth has a God-given capacity and right to
choose. We're born into a world where everything operates by
decision. This is especially true where spiritual things are concerned. In reality, Christianity is really nothing more than a
series of decisions.

For example, Jesus died on the cross so that you might have
forgiveness of sins and inherit eternal life. But that fact does you
absolutely no good unless you make a decision to receive what He

did for you. God is honor-bound to respect and protect your right to choose, even if that means letting you spend eternity in hell.

You can say, "I'm waiting on God." But God is saying, "No, I'm waiting on you. Decide." It's up to you to decide which way you're going to go. Life or death, the choice is yours. Deuteronomy 30:19 says so:

> I have set before you life and death, blessing and cursing: therefore choose life, that both thou and thy seed may live.

The preeminence of man's right to choose is a theme you'll see repeated throughout the entire Bible. Truly, we all live in "the valley of decision."

MAN THE CHOOSER

How much does God's Word have to say about the power of your choices? A lot. From Genesis to Revelation, you'll find the Scriptures emphasizing different aspects of mankind's decision-making power. Let's look at just a few:

> And if it seem evil unto you to serve the LORD, choose you this day whom ye will serve; whether the gods which your fathers served that were on the other side of the flood, or the gods of the Amorites, in whose land ye dwell: but as for me and my house, we will serve the LORD.
>
> —*Joshua 24:15*

Go and say unto David, Thus saith the LORD, I offer thee three things; choose thee one of them, that I may do it unto thee.

—*2 Samuel 24:12*

A change in status, whether good or bad, always begins with a decision. Whatever direction you're moving, it's a result of past choices:

Let us choose to us judgment: let us know among ourselves what is good.

—*Job 34:4*

What man is he that feareth the LORD? Him shall he teach in the way that he shall choose.

—*Psalm 25:12*

For that they hated knowledge, and did not choose the fear of the LORD.

—*Proverbs 1:29*

Envy thou not the oppressor, and choose none of his ways.

—*Proverbs 3:31*

❋ *A change in status, whether good or bad, always begins with a decision.*

Are you facing a seemingly enormous problem? No amount of prayer, no amount of counseling—and all the spiritual activity in the world won't make a bit of difference until you decide to do things God's way, according to His Word and the leading of His Spirit. Nothing will make your situation better until you make that choice.

> ❀ *All the spiritual activity in the world won't make a bit of difference until you decide to do things God's way.*

Butter and honey shall he eat, that he may know to refuse the evil, and choose the good.

—*Isaiah 7:15*

For thus saith the LORD unto the eunuchs that keep my sabbaths, and choose the things that please me, and take hold of my covenant.

—*Isaiah 56:4*

Choosing rather to suffer affliction with the people of God, than to enjoy the pleasures of sin for a season. . . .

—*Hebrews 11:25*

I have chosen the way of truth: thy judgments have I laid before me.

—*Psalm 19:30*

A QUALITY DECISION

Faith's power to change your circumstances is not going to operate in your life until you decide you are going to live by faith in God. This requires what I call a *quality decision*. A quality decision is one on which you're willing to stake your very life. It's not an "ought to" decision. It's not a "probably" decision. It's a determined, resolved "I will" decision to trust God and His Word over any circumstance.

Why is such a firm exercise of your will so important? Because nobody moves into the reality of God's answers without passing through the door of a determined decision. Decisiveness is the door to receiving the promises of God.

> ❋ *Decisiveness is the door to receiving the promises of God.*

Waiting on the other side of that door is Almighty God—ready and willing to back you up with all of heaven's power. He will move earth and sky on behalf of someone who has purposed to do things by the Book. You make the decision—God will back you up.

Until you make a quality decision to do things God's way, He cannot and will not do a thing for you. You have to get fed up with where you are. You have to tear the Devil's yoke of bondage off your neck and throw it down. All of heaven is waiting for your quality decision! Are you going to choose to continue to live with that problem and let it defeat you, or are you going to make a firm, unwavering decision to overcome it?

Making this decision is an essential step in the divine order of faith, and it's precisely where many people stumble. They're halfhearted or wishy-washy in their commitment to win. This wimpy sort of resolve will never move you to the place of victory. You've got to say, "I'm coming out of this situation. I'm coming out by the power of God, and I'm coming out by His Word. I've made my decision, and from this point forward nothing is going to change my mind." When you've made that kind of quality decision, then and only then are you ready to move on to the next step toward victory.

∽ Think about It ∾

1. What is one of the main ways we are made in the image of God?

2. What theme is found in Deuteronomy 30:19 and repeated throughout the Bible?

3. Why is it so important to God that He preserve our free will in all things?

4. Review the Scriptures on decision making given in this chapter. What is God telling you about the power of choice?

5. Why is choosing God's way sometimes scarier or more difficult than going your own way?

6. Why must we "fear the Lord" before He will give us His wisdom and guidance?

7. What are some steps you can take to understand God's will in your life?

8. What should you do when you are not sure what choice to make?

9. How will you know when you are making the right choice?

10. Why must we choose God again and again? What difference does it make?

11. When you determine to operate according to God's Word, what happens?

12. How do people miss the blessings and power of God?

✐ Reflect on It ✐

And if it seem evil unto you to serve the LORD, choose you this day whom ye will serve; whether the gods which your fathers served that were on the other side of the flood, or the gods of the Amorites, in whose land ye dwell: but as for me and my house, we will serve the LORD.

—Joshua 24:15

My prayer in the power of the Word:

_____

_____

_____

_____

_____

For thus saith the LORD unto the eunuchs that keep my sabbaths, and choose the things that please me, and take hold of my covenant; even unto them will I give in mine house and within my walls a place and a name better than of sons and of daughters: I will give them an everlasting name, that shall not be cut off.

—Isaiah 56:4–5

My prayer in the power of the Word:

_____

_____

_____

_____

_____

He hath sent me to bind up the brokenhearted, to proclaim liberty to the captives, and the opening of the prison to them that are bound.

—*Isaiah 61:1*

My prayer in the power of the Word:

_____

_____

_____

_____

_____

Do It

1. Do a word study in your Bible on the words *choose, choice,* and *decision*. Think about how decisive God is. Then think about how decisive you are in comparison. Record your thoughts in your journal.

2. Read the statement you wrote in Step 1 when you identified your problem. Did you do anything to bring that problem on yourself? If so, make a list in your journal of all the choices you made, conscious or not, that brought you to where you are now. Think about what decisions you could have made instead. How can this help you overcome your problem? How can this help you avoid similar problems in the future?

3. Think about the choice you need to make. What is difficult about making that decision? What are you afraid of? Make a list in your journal. Then consider what you wrote. Are your fears rational? What can you do to minimize your apprehension about making this choice? Ask God to give you concrete ideas, and write them down. Then commit to doing what you've written.

4. Practice making conscious choices to do things God's way. Start in the little things, and over time it will become a habit, making it easier to choose God's way in the big

things. Be kind to the clerk at the grocery store. Approach your children with more patience. Decline to participate in gossip. If you catch yourself being critical of others, choose compassion instead. If somebody hurts or offends you, forgive that person immediately. If you find yourself feeling envious or prideful, ask God to remove that from you. Begin now to regularly make intentional decisions.

5. In one simple sentence, write down a choice you will make today. Use strong, present-tense action words. Be decisive, be specific, and be prepared to claim your victory!

6. Find one person whom you trust. Walk up to that person and say in your most authoritative voice: "I've made my decision and from this point forward, nothing can change my mind. By the power of God I'm going to _____." Note how the person responds. Is she surprised? Is she proud of you? Has she heard this before? What can you tell this person about why this time it's different?

Step Three:
Find Your "Title Deed"

> Now faith is the substance of things hoped for, the evidence of things not seen.
>
> —*Hebrews 11:1*

Evidence. Our entire system of justice is based on it. When a district attorney brings you into court to accuse you of a crime, he'd better have convincing evidence to support his claim. He must produce fingerprints, witnesses, or some other type of evidence that indicates your guilt. Otherwise, the judge will throw the case out of court and have a stern talk with that DA!

In the same way, evidence is required of you when you approach the spiritual court of heaven. If you're going to claim that healing, provision, peace, safety, or some other spiritual blessing belongs to you, you'd better have some solid biblical evidence to back up your claim. In other words, you'd better have faith.

The fact is, most of the time when Christians pray and attempt to claim their right to victory over a certain problem, they come to heaven's court without a shred of evidence to substantiate their claims. As a result, the Devil and his crew just laugh and continue to commit their crimes.

This brings us to the third step in God's divine order of faith. Once you've identified your problem and determined in your heart that you're going to overcome it by faith in God and His Word, the next step is to go to God's Word and find a promise that speaks to your particular situation. That promise is your legal evidence and your "title deed" to the power and provision of Almighty God.

A title deed is a document that establishes possession of property.[1] If anyone questions whether or not you own your home, car, boat, or any other property, all you have to do is show them your title deed. That is legal proof that you own your property. Your title deed settles it.

The Word of God contains your title deed to all the blessings of God. And believe me, the Enemy will come along to question your ownership of those blessings. Your title deed is the evidence of what God has given you, what is legally yours. You need to know your title deed to whatever the Devil is trying to steal, kill, or destroy.

> ❁ *The Word of God contains your title deed to all the blessings of God.*

FIND YOUR EVIDENCE

Now faith is the substance of things hoped for, the evidence of things not seen. For by it the elders obtained a good report. Through faith we understand that the worlds were framed by the word of God, so that things which are seen were not made of things which do appear.

—Hebrews 11:1–3

In a previous chapter we talked about faith being a literal substance—a very real spiritual material. Now let's look at the second part of Hebrews 11:1. Faith is also "the evidence of *things not seen*" (emphasis mine).

Notice that faith is the "evidence of things." Most of the time when you are praying, you are asking and believing for a certain "thing." That thing might be money to pay your bills. It might be a new or better car. The thing you need could be healing or the salvation of a friend or loved one. Whatever it is, faith is the evidence of it. You are not going to obtain any *thing* without faith evidence.

> ❁ *You are not going to obtain any* thing *without faith evidence.*

Notice that the Bible says that faith is the evidence of "things *not seen*" (emphasis mine). That's part of what makes faith seem like such foolishness to the natural mind (see 1 Corinthians 2:14).

The unrenewed mind says, "Seeing is believing," or "I'll believe it when I see it." But real Bible faith is believers' assurance that a thing is theirs, even though they have never seen it!

The *Amplified Bible*'s translation of this verse sheds further light on this important truth:

> Now, faith is the assurance (the confirmation, the title deed) of the things [we] hope for, being the proof of things [we] do not see and the conviction of their reality [faith perceiving as real fact what is not revealed to the senses].
>
> —*Hebrews 11:1* AMP

That word "confirmation" is instructive. Have you ever called to reserve a rental car? You might call the Rent-a-Car company and say, "I want a black Lincoln Town Car next Tuesday." At that point they would say, "Okay, let me give you a confirmation number." That confirmation number is your assurance that a black Lincoln has been set aside for your use. Can you see the car? Of course not. Then how do you know you have one? Because that confirmation number is your evidence of a thing not seen.

What happens if you show up at the Rent-a-Car counter on the appointed day and are told, "I'm sorry, we don't have a car for you"? You can say, "Hold on just a minute! I've got a confirmation number. Here it is. Get me a black Town Car now!"

If I showed you the deed to my house, you wouldn't question for a moment that there really was a house at that address. You may not see the house, but my title deed is ample proof that it exists and it is mine.

Child of God, that's exactly what Hebrews 11:1 is trying to communicate to you. If you've been told you have cancer, you can go to the Word and find, "With his stripes we are healed" (Isaiah 53:5). That's your confirmation number—your title deed to health and healing.

When the doctors say you've got three weeks to live, you can hold up your title deed and say with confidence, "I will live and not die because I'm healed by the stripes of Jesus!" You have the proof, the evidence, of your healing. And every devil in hell has to acknowledge and defer to the strength of your evidence.

If you're in a situation where your bills need to be paid and collectors are calling, you can stand up and say, "Hold it! I'm a tither and a giver, and Philippians 4:19 says my God shall supply all my needs according to His riches in glory by Christ Jesus."

No matter what you need, regardless of how serious your circumstances, if you will hold on to that title deed and have faith in God and His promises, it will surely come to pass. The power of that kind of faith never fails.

BE A DETECTIVE

How do district attorneys obtain the evidence they present in court? They depend on detectives who snoop and search until they find what they're looking for.

You need to do the same thing if you're going to win your case against the Devil and everything he's trying to do to you and your family. You're going to have to get out your Bible and search out the verses that speak directly to your particular situation.

I've had sincere people tell me they are believing God for a miraculous healing. When I ask them what they are basing their faith on, they say, "I'm standing on the Word."

"Yes, but what part of the Word?" I ask.

"Oh, no part in particular. Just the Word in general."

The Word "in general" won't bring your miracle. Your case will be thrown out for lack of evidence. You need specific evidence from the Bible to bring God's power onto the scene, because it is your faith in what He has said in the Book that connects you to His supernatural ability. It is entirely up to you to find what He has said in His Book about your particular problem.

Second Timothy 2:15 says, "Study to shew thyself approved unto God, a workman that needeth not to be ashamed, rightly dividing the word of truth." There's the key: study, study, study! Of course it's not easy. It calls for a commitment of time and concentration. But it's the only way you're ever going to get the evidence you need to win your case.

Why is finding Scriptures that speak to your situation so effective? Because when you locate a Bible verse that promises the thing you need, it energizes your prayer with confidence. First John 5:14–15 says it this way:

> And this is the confidence that we have in him, that, if we ask any thing according to his will, he heareth us: And if we know that he hear us, whatsoever we ask, we know that we have the petitions that we desired of him.

❋ *When you locate a Bible verse that promises the thing you need, it energizes your prayer.*

Notice it doesn't say, "We know we're *going to have* the petitions we desire." It doesn't say that *someday* we will have it. It says, "If we ask . . . we know that we have the petitions we desired of him." That's present tense . . . *now*.

God's Word is His will. His will is His Word. If you see it in your Bible, you can know that it's the expressed, perfect will of God for your life. Then when you pray, you can have confidence that He hears you and will answer.

If you are new to the Bible and don't know how to find specific promises, invest in a good concordance. It will give you a list of Scriptures for every subject you can imagine. Look those Scriptures up and ask the Holy Spirit to reveal God's perfect will for you in the problem you are facing. God's Word for your situation is your title deed to His promises and your victory.

Once you've found your title deed in God's Word, pray and consider the matter settled. In fact, start acting as if you possess the thing you've prayed for, because you do! You have settled it in the spirit realm with God. It is yours. And you can have confidence that it will surely manifest in your life because whatever happens in the natural realm is always first accomplished in the spirit realm.

❋ *Once you've found your title deed in God's Word,*
pray and consider the matter settled.

DOING IT BY THE BOOK

You can't dabble in the Word and expect to get results. You can't just "try it out" for a while to see if the Word works. Effective faith demands a lifestyle in which you abandon yourself to the Bible. It's an all-out commitment to live by the Word, to think by the Word, and to talk by the Word.

You see this type of resolve in the most successful people in the Bible:

Be it according to thy word. (Exodus 8:10)

Israel did according to the word. (Exodus 12:35)

The children of Levi did according to the word. (Exodus 32:28)

Israel did according to the word. (Exodus 39:32)

According to all that the LORD commanded. . . . (Exodus 39:42)

According to all thy commandments. . . . (Deuteronomy 26:13)

According to the word of the LORD they gave him the city. (Joshua 19:50)

They hearkened therefore to the word of the LORD. (1 Kings 12:24)

Taking heed therefore according to thy word. . . . (Psalm 119:9)

Be it unto me according to thy word. (Luke 1:38)

Whatever you do, make sure you do it according to the Word. It's your evidence and title deed to everything you need.

HOLD ON TO YOUR EVIDENCE

Once you've found your title deed, hold on with bulldog tenacity and don't let go. At first it may seem as if nothing is happening. In fact, your outward circumstances may even get worse. But no matter what happens, don't let go of your evidence. The writer of Hebrews put it this way:

> Cast not away therefore your confidence, which hath great recompence of reward.
>
> —*Hebrews 10:35*

Child of God, if you're sick, get the evidence of your healing from God's Word. If you're lacking finances, get your evidence of prosperity. If you're in bondage to habits, get your evidence of power over sin. If you're depressed, get your evidence of deliverance.

No matter how hard it gets or how grim your circumstances appear, regardless of what the doctors, bankers, or neighbors say—hold on to that title deed. God will be faithful to come through for you right on time.

Regardless of what you're facing today, there is a promise in God's Word that addresses your need, a promise you can stake your very life on. Find it; then get ready to move on to the next step in God's divine order.

∽ Think about It ∽

1. Look up the word *evidence* in the dictionary. Then meditate on Hebrews 11:1. Compare our modern court procedure with heavenly court procedure.

2. Explain what a title deed is. What is your title deed to all the blessings of God?

3. What is faith the evidence of, and what does that mean to you personally?

4. Why does faith seem foolish to many people?

5. Why won't the Word "in general" work in the court of heaven?

6. Read 1 John 5:14–15 again. When you pray according to God's will, what happens to you? After you pray, what should be your attitude?

7. How do you know you have the "right" to claim the Bible's promises as your own?

8. How much of your life must you surrender to God's Word in order to be successful?

9. Give three examples of people in the Bible who lived according to the Word of God. What was their evidence?

10. Hebrews 10:35 makes it clear that if you hold on to your evidence, what will happen?

11. How powerful and important is the Word of God? How do you know?

12. What is the one thing you must do in order to claim God's promises as your own?

✐ Reflect on It ✐

Now faith is the substance of things hoped for, the evidence of things not seen. For by it the elders obtained a good report. Through faith we understand that the worlds were framed by the word of God, so that things which are seen were not made of things which do appear.

—Hebrews 11:1–3

My prayer in the power of the Word:

_____

_____

_____

_____

_____

And this is the confidence that we have in him, that, if we ask any thing according to his will, he heareth us: And if we know that he hear us, whatsoever we ask, we know that we have the petitions that we desired of him.

—1 John 5:14–15

My prayer in the power of the Word:

_____

_____

_____

_____

_____

And whatsoever ye shall ask in my name, that will I do,
that the Father may be glorified in the Son. If ye shall ask
any thing in my name, I will do it.

—John 14:13–14

My prayer in the power of the Word:

_____

_____

_____

_____

_____

✧ Do It ✧

1. Spend time in prayer confessing your sins and expressing your repentance. Ask the Holy Spirit to reveal any hidden areas of sin. If you have been struggling or rebellious in a particular aspect of sin, spend extra time praying about it, giving it up to God, and asking Him to free you from your rebellion. Seek God's heart and will for you as you prepare to claim His promises. Do this for as long as it takes to sense that your heart is right with God and you are at peace with Him. Only then should you continue with the process of finding your evidence and claiming His promises.

2. Have you made a promise that you haven't fulfilled? Most of us have pledged something to someone that we just haven't found the time to deliver on. Did you tell your kids you'd take them to the zoo? Did you say to a friend, "Let's get together—I'll call you"? Did you offer to watch your neighbor's children so she could go to a movie? Did you promise to return a book or CD that you've borrowed? Now is the time to write down every outstanding promise you've made and make plans to deliver immediately. Make those phone calls, send those e-mails—whatever you need to do. Live up to your word. Note in your journal how it feels to deliver something you've promised, and what happens in your relationships as a result

of your doing so. Does this help you understand how much God loves to deliver on His promises to us?

3. Give a gift to someone just because you love her. It can be something small and simple. You can do it anonymously, if you like. Pay attention to your thoughts and feelings as you choose the gift, wrap it, and deliver it. Do you find yourself focusing intently on that person? Are you eager to choose something she'll truly enjoy? Are you excited to see her reaction? Imagine God feeling this way when He gives you gifts. How does that change your perception of Him?

4. Search your Bible for believers who stepped out and took risks based on a Word or promise from God. Make a list of their names and what they did. How does this knowledge inspire or encourage you in your situation?

5. Look at the statement you wrote in your journal during Step 1, identifying your problem. Read over your quality decision from Step 2. Think about your situation in terms of what you'd like to ask for from God. What do you need from Him? In your journal, make a list of words that relate to your need. Do you need healing? Peace? Freedom? Wisdom? Greater prosperity? Come up with as many words as you can that capture what you'd like to receive from God.

6. Set aside a specific amount of time to spend with God and His Word over the next several days. Get out your

concordance and, using your list of words from the previous question, begin searching the Bible for promises that apply to your situation. As you find verses that speak to your heart, jot them down in your journal. Spend as much time or as many days as you need to do this. You will probably find that it's fun being a Bible detective! When you feel you've exhausted your list of words, look over the verses you've copied down. Pray through each of them, and ask for God's leading to decide which of these will be your title deed. Write your title deed down on a separate piece of paper and post it where you can see it every day: on your refrigerator, your bathroom mirror, your computer, in your car—or all of the above! Better yet, carry it in your purse or in your wallet so that it's always with you. Focus on it several times a day, and begin to claim it as your own. Make sure you save the list of the other verses you found, too. You will need them in Step 4.

Step Four:
Listen to the Word

Hear, O my son, and receive my sayings.
—*Proverbs 4:10*

So far you've been given the first three steps of the supernatural sequence that will move you from any problem or crisis to a miraculous solution. They are: (1) identify the problem, (2) make a quality decision to overcome the problem by faith in God and His Word, and (3) find your title deed to an answer in God's Word.

The next link in this chain of victory involves understanding the importance of *hearing* God's Word. I cannot overstate how vital a role hearing plays in your spiritual life. Your ears are one of only two natural gateways to your spirit. Your eyes are the other. And as far as the things of God are concerned, there is no receiving without hearing. A quick reading of Revelation, chapters 2 and 3, will illustrate just how serious Jesus is about our hearing His words. Seven different times in two chapters He says:

He that hath an ear, let him hear what the Spirit saith unto the churches.

—*Revelation 2:7, 11, 17, 29; 3:6, 13, 22*

I'd say the Lord thinks it's important for us to listen to what He has to say, wouldn't you?

THE ACT OF HEARING

Hearing is nothing more than receiving through the "ear gate." However, biblical hearing involves more than mere listening. It requires attentiveness, belief, and obedience as well. For example, Proverbs 4:10 ties *hearing* directly to *receiving:*

Hear, O my son, and receive my sayings; and the years of thy life shall be many.

—*Proverbs 4:10*

The promise of a long, good life is for those who both hear and receive God's wise sayings. "Receive" is another way of saying "obey." If you're not determined to obey what God has spoken, you haven't really received it. James tells us to be "doers of the word, and not hearers only" (James 1:22).

Proverbs 4:10 tells us that the ultimate result of hearing and receiving is long life. At the end of hearing and receiving, there is always a harvest. It's an unstoppable spiritual progression. Hear! Receive! Harvest!

> ❋ *At the end of hearing and receiving, there is always a harvest.*

Proverbs 8:34 gives us another view of this truth:

Blessed is the man that heareth me, watching daily at my gates, waiting at the posts of my doors.

Blessing is always a result of true hearing, and to be blessed means to be empowered to prosper. Genuine biblical prosperity deals with much more than money. It involves abundance, peace, and increase in every area of human existence.

In a very real sense, prosperity is the ability to control your circumstances instead of your circumstances' controlling you. Hearing the Word of God gives you that kind of power. What you hear, believe, and obey determines your ability to overcome a situation directed toward you by the forces of hell.

> ❋ *Prosperity is the ability to control your circumstances instead of your circumstances' controlling you.*

When Satan tries to put sickness on you and whispers, "You're going to die," there are two ways you can respond. If you've been spending your time listening to the doctor's bad reports and your relatives' stories about all the people they know who died of what you have, you might as well get your affairs in order. You're not empowered to take control of anything. You have no promises of God in your heart to stand on and defeat the Enemy. But if you immerse yourself in the Word of God regarding your health and healing, you will have the power to drive the Devil and his lying symptoms out.

SUBTLE SOUNDS

I remember the day I got a vivid lesson on the subtle power of what we hear. Another pastor and I were enjoying a great time of fellowship in a local pizza parlor. We were talking about the Word and the goodness of God. We sat there for several hours, completely caught up in talking about the things of the Lord. While we were there, someone played an ungodly secular song on the jukebox several times.

As we walked out to our cars later, we both started singing the chorus of that song! We hadn't even really listened to the song, yet it had penetrated our spirits and was now lingering in our consciousnesses. Our mouths automatically started speaking what had been sown in our hearts through the gateway of our ears.

That's why you need to be so selective about what type of conversation you permit yourself to hear. You can't hang around with people who constantly talk about their doubt and unbelief without being adversely affected.

You may say, "Oh, I just let that stuff go in one ear and out the other." But that's impossible! Just as I ended up singing a song I wasn't even listening to, you'll end up singing your friend's song of doubt and unbelief when times get tough. That which enters your ear penetrates your heart and will eventually end up coming out of your mouth.

✾ *That which enters your ear penetrates your heart and will eventually end up coming out of your mouth.*

You simply must guard your ears. The words you habitually listen to will become what you ultimately believe. Association brings assimilation.

FAITH COMETH

One of the most frequently cited verses of Scripture concerning faith is Romans 10:17. Let's look at it in context:

How then shall they call on him in whom they have not believed? And how shall they believe in him of whom they have not heard? And how shall they hear without a preacher? And how shall they preach, except they be sent? As it is written, How beautiful are the feet of them that preach the gospel of peace, and bring glad tidings of good things! But they have not all obeyed the gospel. For Esaias saith, Lord, who hath believed our report? So then faith cometh by hearing, and hearing by the word of God.

—*Romans 10:14–17*

"Faith cometh by hearing, and hearing by the word of God." We've heard it and said it so often that it has almost become a cliché in many Christian circles. But what does this familiar statement really mean? Let's look at the *Amplified Bible* for more light on these verses:

> But how are people to call upon Him Whom they have not believed [in Whom they have no faith, on Whom they have no reliance]? And how are they to believe in Him [adhere to, trust in, and rely upon Him] of Whom they have never heard? And how are they to hear without a preacher? And how can men [be expected to] preach unless they are sent? As it is written, How beautiful are the feet of those who bring glad tidings! [How welcome is the coming of those who preach the good news of His good things!] [Isa. 52:7.] But they have not all heeded the Gospel; for Isaiah says, Lord who has believed (had faith in) what he has heard from us? [Isa. 53:1.] So faith comes by hearing [what is told], and what is heard comes by the preaching [of the message that came from the lips] of Christ (the Messiah Himself). (AMP)

When verse 14 asks, "How are they to believe in Him . . . of Whom they have never heard?" (AMP), it introduces a very important spiritual truth. You can't believe in or ask for something that you've never heard preached.

Have you ever noticed that in churches where salvation is never preached, nobody gets saved? And in churches where they preach salvation but never preach healing, people get saved but no one gets healed. Is it any wonder there are so many people who can't pay their bills in churches where the pastor never preaches that it's God's will for believers to prosper?

If you've never heard that God is your Deliverer, how can you ever be delivered? You can't believe in something you've never heard proclaimed. That's why it is so important that preachers preach the whole Word, from A to Z. As this passage of Scripture asks, "How can the people hear without a preacher?"

> ❊ *You can't believe in something you've never heard proclaimed.*

Then God's Word asks another question: "How can men preach unless they are sent?" Some preachers are sent, commissioned, and ordained by God. Others just go in their own power and strength. When it comes to deciding which preacher you're going to listen to, you've got to know the difference between the "sent" one and the "went" one.

When God sends you to do something, He provides all the necessary equipment and ability to get the job done. If I send my son to the store for groceries, I'm going to give him enough money to buy the things I've asked him to get. The same principle holds true for preachers.

The "went" preacher who takes off on his own initiative because he thinks it's a good idea won't have the equipment he needs because He is preaching on his own initiative and has not been sent by God or anointed by Him to preach. Preachers who are sent by God are anointed by Him to preach.

Why is it one man can get up and preach a sermon with

tremendous, life-changing results in the lives of the hearers, while another will preach the same sermon with no results? It's the difference between the sent one and the went one. The sent one is anointed with the power of the Holy Spirit, and therefore the Holy Spirit reveals God's Word to him (see John 14:26).

That's why you need to be discerning even when it comes to Christian radio and television. Some believers think they're doing a good thing by tuning in to a Christian station and just leaving it on. But in reality a lot of doubt, unbelief, and bad teaching may be bombarding your ears if you do that.

Why is listening to the wrong things dangerous? The Bible says in Proverbs 4:23 that you must guard your heart "with all diligence," because out of your heart come the forces of your life. In other words, whatever you believe in your heart will direct your decisions in life.

> ❈ *Whatever you believe in your heart will direct your decisions in life.*

If you are listening to teachers and preachers who doubt God's Word, you will begin to doubt God's Word in your heart. And doubting God's Word in your heart is the same as not having faith in Him.

Do you see how important it is, again, to be careful what you hear? What you hear determines what you believe in your heart, and what you believe in your heart determines every decision you make in life. What you hear determines your very faith in God because "faith cometh by hearing" (Romans 10:17).

YOU NEED A FRESH HEARING

Let's look at old familiar Romans 10:17 one more time:

So then faith cometh by hearing, and hearing by the word of God.

Please understand what the Word is saying here. It does you no good to hear the Word concerning finances if you have cancer. If you are sick and need faith to get healed, faith comes by hearing the Word of God concerning healing. Likewise, it doesn't help to hear the Word on healing when you need money. Faith for whatever you need comes from hearing and acting on the Word that specifically deals with that particular need.

It's also important to understand that faith doesn't come from "having heard"—past tense. It comes from "hearing"—present tense. Some people think because they heard "With his stripes we are healed" (Isaiah 53:5) many years ago, they have the faith to be healed today. It simply doesn't work that way.

Just because you put gas in your car last month or even last week doesn't mean you have the fuel to get you where you need to go today. Gas to get you to work this week comes by stopping and pumping a fresh tankful.

The memory of yesterday's meal won't strengthen and nourish you for today's activity. You are going to have to have another meal. It may be the same menu you ate yesterday, but you still must eat again.

The same is true of hearing the Word. You need a fresh hearing to receive faith for today's needs. I don't care how many times you've heard a certain verse—you may be able to quote it backwards, forwards, and in your sleep—but you must hear it now for today's problem. For the Word to speak to your present situation, you need to see it in your own Bible, hear it preached by a man or woman of God today, and receive it and believe it in your own heart now.

When sickness tries to attack my body, the first thing I do is get my healing tapes out and start listening to them. I open my Bible, look up all the verses on healing, read them aloud, and preach them to myself until I believe them in my heart. I grab hold of God's promises and eat, drink, sleep, and live them with every ounce of my being.

Faith is not a onetime event. It is a life of trusting God. It is a process that we do over and over again of hearing and believing Him and His Word in our hearts. We will never win a battle on the shells we fired in the last war. When a new enemy comes, it's time to reload. Reloading the gun of faith comes by hearing and hearing by the Word of God.

❊ *Faith is not a onetime event. It is a life of trusting God.*

RECEIVE GOD'S WORD, NOT THE ENEMY'S

Not only is it vital that you hear the Word when you're facing a problem, but it is also important to hear it properly. *How* you receive God's Word has an enormous impact on the results you see. That is precisely what Jesus said in Mark 4:24 right after He gave the parable of the sower and the soils:

And he said unto them, Take heed what ye hear: with what measure ye mete, it shall be measured to you: and unto you that hear shall more be given.

Once again we are warned: "Take heed what you hear." Don't allow just anything to go through the gate of your ears. If you're sick and need healing, whatever you do, don't let your relatives sit around your bed telling you how bad you look. If you are trying to build a prosperous business, don't sit around listening to people talk about how terrible the economy is. Why? Because fear cometh by hearing, and hearing by the word of the Enemy.

> ❈ *Fear cometh by hearing, and hearing by the word of the Enemy.*

Fear is the reciprocal of faith. And as powerful as faith is to do you good, fear is powerful to open you up to harm. Take another look at the last half of that verse:

With what measure ye mete, it shall be measured to you: and unto you that hear shall more be given.

This applies the law of sowing and reaping to the act of hearing the Word of God. The more attention and weight you give to the Word, the more revelation and power you're going to receive. Those who learn to hear well will hear more and more.

In other words, not only will you get results from hearing the Word, but you'll get revelation too! And Jesus said the very gates of hell could not prevail against the rock of personal revelation of God's Word (see Matthew 16:18).

FALL IN LOVE WITH THE WORD

There is no way to overemphasize the importance of hearing, and hearing, and hearing the Word of God. In John 8:47, Jesus tells us, "He that is of God heareth God's words; ye therefore hear them not, because ye are not of God." He's saying, "If you're of God, you will really hear—receive, believe, and live— My Word."

Few things in your Christian walk will benefit you more than simply falling in love with God's Word. Hear the Word as you read it. Hear it on television, tapes, and radio. Hear it preached by an anointed man or woman of God in church. Just hear it.

This is never more vital than when you are facing a problem or need. Go to the Word and find a promise that directly answers that problem. Then hear it, hear it, and hear it some more. It's a powerful and absolutely essential step in God's divine order of faith for getting you from the problem to the answer. Victory is waiting for you!

❧ Think about It ❧

1. What are the two natural gateways to your spirit?

2. Read Revelation, chapters 2 and 3. What does Jesus repeat again and again to the churches?

3. What three things does biblical hearing require of you?

4. Describe biblical prosperity. How does what you hear empower you to prosper—or not?

5. Explain what happened to Pastor Dollar and his minister friend in the restaurant. Why is that significant?

6. What does "association brings assimilation" mean to you?

7. How does faith grow in you? What verse of Scripture gives this answer?

8. Is the whole counsel of God taught in your church? Why is it important to listen to ministers who teach the Bible from A to Z?

9. How is hearing the Word of God like eating when it comes to walking in faith?

10. Discuss the difference between faith and fear. How does fear work? How does faith work?

11. Mark 4:24 applies what law to hearing the Word of God? How does this affect what you receive from God?

12. Name the benefits you enjoy by loving God's Word.

Reflect on It

And He said to them, Be careful what you are hearing. The measure [of thought and study] you give [to the truth you hear] will be the measure [of virtue and knowledge] that comes back to you—and more [besides] will be given to you who hear.

—*Mark 4:24* AMP

My prayer in the power of the Word:

_____

_____

_____

_____

_____

Hear, O my son, and receive my sayings; and the years of thy life shall be many.

—*Proverbs 4:10*

My prayer in the power of the Word:

_____

_____

_____

_____

_____

How then shall they call on him in whom they have not believed? And how shall they believe in him of whom they have not heard? And how shall they hear without a preacher? And how shall they preach, except they be sent? As it is written, How beautiful are the feet of them that preach the gospel of peace, and bring glad tidings of good things! But they have not all obeyed the gospel. For Esaias saith, Lord, who hath believed our report? So then faith cometh by hearing, and hearing by the word of God.

—*Romans 10:14–17*

My prayer in the power of the Word:

_____

_____

_____

_____

_____

_____

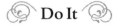 **Do It**

1. Locate a sermon on CD, a book on CD, or a book of the Bible on CD that deals with the problem you are currently facing. Listen to it as much as possible this week.

2. Listen to a sermon at your church or on the radio. Look up the passages discussed and compare your reading of the Bible to what was preached. Is there any discrepancy? How does this exercise improve your understanding of the material? Does it give you more or less confidence in the preaching?

3. Commit to immersing yourself in the Word for a specific number of minutes or hours this week. Then do it. Count everything you do to "hear" the Word: listening to sermons, reading the Bible, listening to Christian music, reading Christian books, or attending Bible study. At the end of the week, review how you did. Was it easier or more difficult than you anticipated?

4. Evaluate your own pollution factor. Look at how much time you spend each week participating in gossip, listening to the radio, watching television, hearing secular music, reading tabloid magazines, or being exposed to any other negative influences. If 1 is "totally pure," and 10 is "completely corrupted," where do you rate yourself on the pollution scale? Where would you like to be?

5. Make a list of ways to improve your personal "hearing" of the Word on a daily basis. Think about both decreasing the negative things you take in and increasing your exposure to the Word and other positive influences. Think of at least five things you can change this week. Write them down and stick to them.

6. Remember that title-deed verse you identified in Step 3? Make sure you are clinging to it, reading it, meditating on it, and praying through it several times a day. Choose at least five of the other verses you found in Step 3, write each one on a piece of paper or index card, and keep them with you. Immerse yourself in these Scriptures.

Step Five:
Meditate on God's Promises

> This book of the law shall not depart out of thy mouth; but thou shalt meditate therein day and night.
>
> —Joshua 1:8

Thus far in our examination of God's divine order of faith, we've established several important biblical truths. One is that God's Word is a spiritual "seed" that has the potential to germinate into whatever you need in your life. Another is that "hearing" is necessary to access that seed. Now we'll see in the Word that the key to planting that seed in your heart, where it can do some good, is *meditation*.

Let me say at the outset that meditation is a subject that is often misunderstood and unnecessarily controversial. When some people hear the word *meditation*, they instantly assume you're talking about some Eastern, mystical, occult practice brought to America by Buddhists or Hindus. Let me assure you, that is not what I am talking about. That kind of meditation is a counterfeit—a perversion of something God created for His people to use.

You see, Satan can't create anything. He can only twist things God created. Certainly there are a lot of people in the occult using Satan's perverted form of meditation, and they are getting perverted, destructive results as they do.

What we will see in this chapter is that *meditation* is a Bible word. We're not taking a tool from the Devil's kingdom and trying to use it for God. We are simply rediscovering a powerful, God-given method for planting the Word deep in our hearts.

In this chapter you'll discover God's purpose for meditation, how your imagination plays a role in getting from the problem to the answer, and how to put meditation and your imagination to godly use to bring phenomenal results in your prayer life.

IMAGINE THAT

At the most basic level, to meditate means to "engage in thought or contemplation." It can also mean to reflect or ponder.[1] To ponder is to think about something, consider it, weigh it in your mind.[2] In addition, real biblical meditation involves the use of the imagination. When you imagine something, you see it in your mind's eye.

I probably don't have to tell you that your imagination can get you into trouble. Unholy imaginations and fantasies have led many a person into dangerous waters. Given the way so many people use their imaginations, the results may often be perverted and wicked. But did you know that using your imagination God's way can get you healed, delivered, and blessed? It can!

> ❀ *Using your imagination God's way can get you healed, delivered, and blessed.*

The imagination, a God-created part of every one of us, is a faculty many of us haven't heard much Bible teaching about. Yet it is a biblical word and one of the most powerful instruments we possess for getting results. Once we uncover God's original purpose for the imagination and begin to use it the way He intended, we'll begin to see astounding, *righteous* results. But only when we use it in the context of God's divine order of faith.

I CAN SEE IT!

How many times have you walked by a department store, looked at a dress or a suit in the window, and remarked, "Wow, I can see myself wearing that"? Has a new car ever passed you and you muttered, "Hey, I can see myself driving something like that"?

The fact is, you really did see yourself driving that car. How? In your mind's eye. Through the faculty of your imagination you were able to see a reality that didn't currently exist. This ability has many spiritual applications.

You may find yourself asking, "But the Bible doesn't say anything about imagination, does it?" Oh, but it does! In fact, it says plenty. One of the first scriptural references to the imagination occurs in Genesis:

And they said, Go to, let us build us a city and a tower, whose top may reach unto heaven; and let us make us a name, lest we be scattered abroad upon the face of the whole earth. And the LORD came down to see the city and the tower, which the children of men builded. And the LORD said, Behold, the people is one, and they have all one language; and this they begin to do: and now nothing will be restrained from them, which they have imagined to do.

—*Genesis 11:4–6*

Here we see a group of ungodly, rebellious people who could accomplish anything they could *imagine* because they were unified in purpose and language. Nothing could hold them back. Their potential was unlimited because they were all imagining the same thing: a blueprint of an incredibly high tower.

The power of unity and imagination got God's immediate attention. In effect, God said, "I've got to put a stop to this. With the blueprint they have imagined, it won't be long until I've got a tower sticking up through my living room!"

Of course I'm being facetious. But the fact remains that because imagination is such a powerful tool, God came down and confounded their language in order to destroy their unity. If you can learn to use your imagination God's way, it will become a formidable weapon for good in your spiritual arsenal.

❋ Your imagination . . . will become a formidable weapon for good in your spiritual arsenal.

Sadly, up to this point many believers have been wasting this awesome, creative tool by meditating on junk, or even worse, things that are unclean and sinful. Yet, as we're about to see, God's plan is for believers to use meditation as a means of overcoming.

GOOD SUCCESS

Now that we have at least a surface understanding of what meditation is, let's find out what the Bible has to say about how to use it:

This book of the law [God's Word] shall not depart out of thy mouth; but thou shalt meditate therein day and night, that thou mayest observe to do according to all that is written therein: for then thou shalt make thy way prosperous, and then thou shalt have good success.

—*Joshua 1:8*

Let's break this verse down and get some understanding of God's purpose for meditation.

First, it says, "This book of the law shall not depart out of thy mouth." God's Law is His Word. His Word is His Law. Therefore the "book of the law," for us, refers to God's Word, the Bible. Here we're told to speak it all the time.

It is vitally important for you to hear yourself speak the Word so that your heart will hear it and believe it. In the previous chapter we saw how what we believe in our hearts determines every decision we make in life, and we want all our decisions to be based on God's Word. If we base all our decisions on God's Word, our lives will be prosperous.

> ❁ *If we base all our decisions on God's Word,*
> *our lives will be prosperous.*

The next part of the verse says, "But thou shalt meditate therein day and night." In other words, take God's Word and ponder it. Dwell on it. Take it and turn it over and around in your mind. Use your imagination to "see" yourself doing that Word. Meditating the Word day and night has the same effect on your heart as speaking the Word.

What does meditating the Word day and night empower you to do? You meditate so you "mayest observe to do according to all that is written therein." It enables you to live what you see in your Bible.

Have you ever been challenged by something you saw in the Word? Have you ever read a biblical command and thought, *I can't do that*? I'd venture to say you have. I've not yet met a believer who got saved and immediately started walking in obedience to everything he saw in Scripture.

When stepping out to a new level of commitment or faith, most of us must face fear. There is the fear that God's Word won't work for us the way it does for others, and the fear that God won't come through. We just can't see ourselves doing the Word.

For instance, when some Christians read Malachi 3:10 and discover they're supposed to tithe, they are gripped with fear. "I can't afford to tithe!" they tell themselves.

The Devil, always willing to lend a helping hand, whispers, "That's right. You can't pay your bills as it is. How are you going to make it if you give 10 percent to God?"

The problem here is that believers can't see themselves tithing and prospering as a result. That's where meditation of the Word comes in. Remember, Joshua 1:8 said that we were to meditate on God's Word day and night "that thou mayest observe to do according to all that is written therein."

That's the key! Meditating on Malachi 3:10 enables you to see it and believe it in your heart, and what you see and believe in your heart determines your decisions in life. Read this verse of Scripture and meditate on it for a few minutes:

Bring ye all the tithes into the storehouse, that there may be meat in mine house, and prove me now herewith, saith the LORD of hosts, if I will not open you the windows of heaven, and pour you out a blessing, that there shall not be room enough to receive it.

As you meditate this verse more and more, you will begin to see the windows of heaven opening up and pouring out blessings as you give to the Lord. The more you meditate the truth of this Scripture, the more real and vivid the image becomes. Eventually you can clearly see yourself tithing and being blessed. Ultimately fear is completely displaced by faith. You're a tither!

This principle works for anything you can find in the Word. The result is always the same:

For then thou shalt make thy way prosperous, and then thou shalt have good success.

Prosperity and success are the inevitable by-products of being a meditator and doer of God's Word.

PLANT IT

The Bible is loaded with promises of blessing and increase for those who will invest time in meditating the Word. You'll find one such promise in Psalm 1:1–3:

Blessed is the man that walketh not in the counsel of the ungodly, nor standeth in the way of sinners, nor sitteth in the seat of the scornful. But his delight is in the law of the Lord; and in his law doth he meditate day and night. And he shall be like a tree planted by the rivers of water, that bringeth forth his fruit in his season; his leaf also shall not wither; and whatsoever he doeth shall prosper.

Who is this well-watered, fruit-bearing person who prospers in everything he does? The one who delights in and meditates on God's Word day and night! He knows how to take the seed of God's Word and plant it deeply in his heart.

If you want a harvest of blessing and victory, you must take the seed (God's Word) out of the bag (the Bible) and plant it in the soil (your heart) through meditation. This is where so many believers miss it. They confuse reading or memorizing Scripture with meditating it. Reading and memorization are wonderful, but they don't plant the seed of the Word in your heart the way meditation does. The first two put the Word in your head; meditation plants it in your heart.

Only when you've planted the seed can you rightfully expect the fruit of the harvest. No farmer in his right mind stands over his fields waiting for a harvest when the seed is still in sacks in the barn. But once he has sown the seed in good soil, he has every reason to expect fruit.

> ❋ *Only when you've planted the seed can you rightfully expect the fruit of the harvest.*

Many Christians are waiting for the Word to produce a harvest in their lives when they've never truly sown it in their hearts. They have heard the Word preached. They have read it many times. They may even have lots of verses memorized. But until God's Word is planted in the fertile soil of an obedient heart, the expectation of harvest is in vain.

HOW TO MEDITATE THE WORD

Okay. Let's get practical. I am going to give you three down-to-earth methods you can start using today to meditate God's Word. The good news is, none of these requires you to sit in the lotus position and hum!

1. Mutter

My hands also will I lift up unto thy commandments, which I have loved; and I will meditate in thy statutes.

—*Psalm 119:48*

Have you ever found yourself walking around muttering something under your breath in a time of stress or irritation? You may not have realized it, but you were practicing a negative form of meditation. The Hebrew word translated "meditate" in Psalm 119:48 can also mean "to talk or speak."[3]

A highly effective method of meditation involves simply speaking a verse (or even a two- or three-word phrase from a verse) to yourself.

"But won't my family and friends think I've lost my marbles if I go around mumbling to myself?" you ask.

They won't after they start seeing the phenomenal change in your life! Besides, speaking to yourself is perfectly biblical. Paul even suggests it:

Be filled with the Spirit; *speaking to yourselves* in psalms and hymns and spiritual songs, singing and making melody in your heart to the Lord.

—*Ephesians 5:18–19, emphasis mine*

❋ *Speaking to yourself is perfectly biblical.*

There you have it. It's in the New Testament. Speaking or singing the Word to yourself is an excellent way to meditate the things of God.

2. Talk

A second way to meditate the Word is to just plain speak it out. That's the basic meaning of the word "meditate" we read in Joshua 1:8. Speaking the Word and its principles out loud—to God, to yourself, or to another person—has a powerful effect on your heart. As you can see in the following verses, words and meditation are closely linked (emphasis mine):

I will *meditate* also of all thy work, and *talk* of thy doings.

—*Psalm 77:12*

Let the *words* of my mouth, and the *meditation* of my heart, be acceptable in thy sight, O LORD, my strength, and my redeemer.

—*Psalm 19:14*

> My mouth shall *speak* of wisdom; and the *meditation* of my
> heart shall be of understanding.
>
> —*Psalm 49:3*

If you and I go to lunch and talk about God's faithfulness to meet all our needs, that conversation stirs up the Word within you and plants more of it in your heart. That works in the negative too. If we sit and talk about how big a failure you are, then it won't be long until you start expecting failure, because seeds of failure have been sown in your heart. Failure has been your meditation.

This is why God is so opposed to sins of the tongue: gossip, backbiting, slander, and the like. Those words are a form of meditation that sink into your heart like poison. "The words of a talebearer are as wounds, and they go down into the innermost parts of the belly [heart]" (Proverbs 18:8).

3. Muse

The third method of effective meditation is the one more commonly associated with it. It is musing over or pondering something from the Word. It's the type of meditation described in Psalm 143:5 (emphasis mine):

> I remember the days of old; I *meditate* on all thy works; I
> *muse* on the work of thy hands.

I liken this kind of meditation to squeezing juice out of an orange. Take a single phrase such as "By His stripes I am healed," and ponder it over and over again until it becomes absolutely real on the inside of you. Squeeze until there's not one drop left.

THE REWARDS ARE WORTH THE EFFORT

Make no mistake about it: this requires considerable effort and self-discipline. There is no lazy way into the deep things of God. Far too many Christians today have developed a welfare mentality where spiritual things are concerned. They want everything cooked in the microwave and served on a platter!

Yes it's hard, but the rewards are great. I challenge you to try the things I've talked about here for seven days. There's no question in my mind that it will revolutionize your spiritual life. You'll experience more power, more answered prayer, more revelation . . . more everything.

> ❋ *You'll experience more power, more answered prayer, more revelation . . . more everything.*

Still, only a handful of Christians ever muster the energy to pay the price for such abundant life. Instead, all too many go begging God for success or healing or whatever it is they need. All the while, the key to the storehouse of heaven—their Bible—is in their hands.

If your response right now is to say, "I'm still not sure I really understand how to meditate," then permit me to bring it right down to where you live. Go to the Scripture and find a verse or passage that addresses a current need. Spend fifteen or twenty minutes meditating on it. Say it quietly to yourself. Ponder it. Consider it. Close your eyes and see yourself acting on or experiencing that Scripture.

Throughout the day, turn to your spouse or friend and make a declaration based on that Scripture (e.g., "God is supplying all my needs according to His riches in glory"). Continue to ponder the verse or phrase as you lay down at night. Your spirit will continue to soak in revelation even while you sleep.

When you wake up, take the same Scripture and start the process again. Mutter it to yourself. Say it to others. Muse on it at every opportunity. As you do, that truth will become more and more alive in your spirit, and that seed will be planted more deeply in your heart.

If you will really give this approach a try, you'll find it to be the most powerful thing you've ever done. Sure, it takes self-discipline. Yes, it requires concentration and commitment. But the rewards are abundant life, victory, health, prosperity, success, and the most precious reward of all—greater intimacy with your heavenly Father.

◌ Think about It ◌

1. What is the key to firmly establishing or "planting" the Word of God in your heart? Who created this key?

2. What are the differences between biblical meditation and meditation used in Eastern religions and occult practices?

3. Discuss the powerful cause and effect of using the imagination—in a godly way and an ungodly way.

4. Read Genesis 11:4–6. Why were the people successful in their initial plans to build the Tower of Babel?

5. In order to be successful in life, how often should you meditate on God's Word? Speak God's Word?

6. Explain how fear is replaced with faith through meditation on God's Word. Give an example.

7. Discuss the difference between reading or memorizing the Word and meditating the Word.

8. What did the apostle Paul mean when he instructed believers to "pray without ceasing" (1 Thessalonians 5:17)?

9. What is the best way to keep your mind from wandering when you meditate?

10. What does it mean to "mutter," and how do you do it?

11. Discuss the power of the "talk it" method of meditation. Why are your spoken words so impactful? Why does God oppose gossip, backbiting, slander, and the like?

12. Why does "musing" require self-discipline?

✎ Reflect on It ✎

This book of the law [God's Word] shall not depart out of
thy mouth; but thou shalt meditate therein day and night,
that thou mayest observe to do according to all that is written therein: for then thou shalt make thy way prosperous,
and then thou shalt have good success.

—*Joshua 1:8*

My prayer in the power of the Word:

_____

_____

_____

_____

_____

Blessed is the man that walketh not in the counsel of the
ungodly, nor standeth in the way of sinners, nor sitteth in
the seat of the scornful. But his delight is in the law of the
LORD; and in his law doth he meditate day and night. And
he shall be like a tree planted by the rivers of water, that
bringeth forth his fruit in his season; his leaf also shall not
wither; and whatsoever he doeth shall prosper.

—*Psalm 1:1–3*

My prayer in the power of the Word:

_____

_____

_____

_____

_____

Let the words of my mouth, and the meditation of my heart, be acceptable in thy sight, O LORD, my strength, and my redeemer.

—Psalm 19:14

My prayer in the power of the Word:

_____

_____

_____

_____

_____

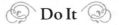

Do It

1. Locate each verse in the Psalms that contains the word *meditate*. Copy the verses onto a separate piece of paper so that you have a page full of verses referring to meditation. Keep it next to your bed or tape it to your bathroom mirror. Pray through these verses at least twice a day for a week or more. See if this helps cement into your mind and heart the importance of daily meditation.

2. Once you become practiced at meditation, you may want to talk about it with others. Research different kinds of meditation, using the Internet or books at the library or bookstore. How many types can you identify? How are these methods distinguished? What does each promise to those who practice it? Finally, in what very important ways are these different from biblical meditation? Make a list or outline in your journal, and study it until you are able to discuss meditation fluently with anyone who is interested. You might want to purposely engage some friends in conversation about it, just for practice.

3. Organize a Scripture meditation group at your church. Seek out others who are interested in meditating. Arrange a meditation gathering of four to ten people, once a week or every two weeks. Choose a Scripture that the entire

group can meditate upon. Have each person share her thoughts with the group.

4. What do you generally meditate on during the day: Winning the lottery? Your loneliness? Anger at your noisy neighbors? Make a list in your journal of the places your mind usually goes. Do you need to change your habits of thinking and how you use your imagination? For each of your typical daydreams, choose a Scripture that you want to replace it with. For example, if you imagine taking revenge on your annoying neighbors, you could replace those negative thoughts with Psalm 4:4 (NIV): "In your anger do not sin." Consciously replace ungodly thinking with the verse you choose for your specific issue. Note the results in your journal.

5. Identify a Scripture that has previously challenged you— one that represents an area of fear. Perhaps it is a proverb against gossip or an admonishment from Jesus to be pure even in your thoughts. Copy down the Scripture, then locate other verses that can enable you to overcome that particular fear. Meditate on them for one week using one or more of the techniques suggested in this chapter. Keep a daily journal of your thinking and emotions. At the end of the week, share the results with a Christian friend or mentor.

6. Meditate on your title-deed verse for a few minutes every day. How is this helping you move toward claiming victory over the problem that plagues you?

Step Six:
Harness the Power of Confession

> For with the heart man believeth unto righteous-
> ness; and with the mouth confession is made unto
> salvation.
>
> —*Romans 10:10*

The sixth step in God's infallible formula for getting you from the problem to the solution is confession. You may be thinking, *Oh, I know all about that confession stuff. It doesn't work for me.* If you think that, you're not alone. People who have heard and received good faith teaching get hung up and frustrated in this area more than any other. The reason is simple.

As I've been saying throughout this book, there is an established, God-ordained order to the things of faith. You simply cannot scramble God's divine order of faith in any way you please and expect to get results. Nor can you pick and choose among these ten steps as if you were in a cafeteria line.

This is doubly true when it comes to confession. So many believers grab on to one little piece of something they hear a teacher like Kenneth Hagin or Kenneth Copeland say regarding confessing what they desire without hearing the whole teaching. Then they run out and start saying, "I have a new car," four hundred times a day—and get irritated when nothing happens after a week.

Is confession a powerful tool? Yes! Can it bring you tremendous supernatural results? Absolutely! But only when preceded and followed by the proper steps in God's order. Let's discover how to harness the awesome power of confession—the Bible way.

FIRST THINGS FIRST

Before we move on to learning how confession is used, let's find out what it is. Defined simply, confession is using the mouth to bring forth. It is more than just saying something. It means to declare a thing in order to establish or confirm it. True confession is an authoritative spiritual proclamation.

A good way to think about effective confession is in terms of firing a gun. A gun that fires blanks sounds the same as one that fires real bullets. They both go "boom!" Yet one is effective; the other just makes noise. If you've got a snake in your yard, you can fire blanks at it all day long and never kill the thing. However, one real bullet will take care of that slimy serpent in no time.

That's why so many Christians have gotten frustrated with confession. The Devil (a serpent) is loose in their finances, health, or family. They are firing the gun of confession—they are saying the right words—yet nothing is happening. Why? They're firing blanks. The gun of confession hasn't been loaded with the right ammunition.

This explains why one person can say, "That car is mine, in the name of Jesus" and get it, while another says the exact same thing but is still taking the bus to work.

EFFECTIVE CONFESSION

Make no mistake about it—words are powerful. Hebrews 11:3 tells us, "The worlds were framed [built] by the word of God." Read the first two chapters of Genesis and you'll see that this is true. For example, Genesis 1:3 says:

And God said, Let there be light: and there was light.

You'll see that phrase, "And God said," repeated again in verses 6, 9, 11, 14, 20, 24, 26, 28, and 29. Each time God wanted to create something new, He *said* something. Don't try to tell me words aren't important! I know from the Word of God that they are creative and powerful.

But words must be based on an underlying faith. Take a look at Romans 10:10:

For with the heart man believeth unto righteousness; and with the mouth confession is made unto salvation.

Consider carefully the order of that verse: it is with your heart that you believe, *then* with your mouth that you confess. We confess what is already true in our hearts. If confession is the gun, words based on an already present inner reality are the bullets. You speak what is real in your heart, what your heart fully possesses. And the gunpowder that fills and propels those bullets is the substance of faith, of course! You know in your heart that what you are confessing is already a reality.

> ✸ *[Words] are creative and powerful.*

This is how all these forces and vehicles interact to produce results, and this is why it is so important to have things in the proper order before you go "shooting your mouth off." Far too often we've hurried to fire the gun of confession without doing what is necessary to load it with a clear inner image (the bullet) and to fill that image with faith (the gunpowder). Other times we've had a loaded gun (a clear inner image and faith) but have neglected to pull the trigger through the exercise of confession.

Getting all of these elements together is not as difficult as it may seem. In fact, if you follow the steps we've outlined thus far, you're already set to take aim and fire.

BUILDING A CLEAR INNER IMAGE

If you ever want to start seeing what you say, you're going to have to learn to create it in your heart first. How do you do that? By diligently doing what we learned in the previous step: meditating the appropriate parts of God's Word.

❋ If you ever want to start seeing what you say, you're going to have to learn to create it in your heart first.

Meditating the Word of God builds a clear image in your heart of the thing for which you are believing. Say, for instance, you need healing. If you will begin meditating on what God's Word has to say about healing—muttering, speaking, and musing, "By His stripes I am healed"—eventually an image of a healed you will begin to take shape in your heart. Once that happens, then and only then will you get the healing out of your heart and into the physical realm of your body through the instrument of confession.

If you've been confessing that all your needs are met in Christ Jesus, but your phone's been disconnected, your electricity has been cut off, and they are carrying your furniture away, perhaps it's because you've never really taken the time to build a clear image of "all-sufficiency" in your heart.

Your mouth's confession and your heart's meditation must go hand in hand for your faith to be released and God's power to invade your situation. One won't work independently of the other. So before you begin confessing God's Word over your problem, make certain you have a real, solid picture of it in your heart.

❋ Your mouth's confession and your heart's meditation must go hand in hand for your faith to be released and God's power to invade your situation.

TIMING IS EVERYTHING

The most common mistake Christians make in the area of confession is failing to wait until the gun is fully loaded before squeezing the trigger. God gives us a great illustration of the power of waiting in Joshua, chapter 6, in which Israel is preparing to take the walled city of Jericho. If you are familiar with the account, you'll remember that God instructed Joshua to have Israel march around the city once a day for six days, and on the seventh day, they were to march around the city seven times. Furthermore, He commanded them to be silent as they walked:

> And Joshua had commanded the people, saying, Ye shall not shout, nor make any noise with your voice, neither shall any word proceed out of your mouth, until the day I bid you shout; then shall ye shout.
>
> —*Joshua 6:10*

Why do you think God had the Israelites march around silently for six days before He would allow them to let go a victory shout? So they would meditate as they marched. With each passing day they developed a clearer inner image of those walls lying on the ground and that city under their control. By the seventh day, when Joshua gave the order to shout, their confession was so loaded with faith's substance that it literally blew those massive walls down.

Seven is a biblical number of completion or perfection.[1] What God is saying here is, "Don't open your mouth until your meditation of My Word is complete." Once the reality of God's promise is more real in your heart than your outward circumstances, you can't help but shout your victory. That's when the walls of whatever is opposing you will crumble like sand.

I've experienced this personally. When I was diagnosed with meningitis, the first thing I did was put my healing tapes on and get my healing Scriptures out. At that point I wasn't making any bold confessions. I just kept my mouth shut and meditated. I muttered and mused those healing Scriptures until I was so full of the reality of healing that it was coming out of my hair. Then, when I knew that I knew it was real, I stood right up in the middle of my bed and shouted, *"I am healed!"*

My symptoms didn't disappear that very instant, but that didn't matter. I knew I was healed. And, of course, I was. My healing manifested in my physical body very quickly. The key was doing the hard work of meditation before moving on to the step of proclaiming my confession.

SUMMING UP THE
HEART-MOUTH CONNECTION

Child of God, the Lord created your heart and your mouth to be married. When you try to use one independently of the other, it's like a type of adultery. That's precisely what many of us have been doing in the area of confession.

Let's return to Romans 10:9–10, because this linkage of heart and mouth is never seen more clearly than in these verses (emphasis mine):

That if thou shalt *confess with thy mouth* the Lord Jesus, and shalt *believe in thine heart* that God hath raised him from the dead, thou shalt be saved. For *with the heart man believeth* unto righteousness; and *with the mouth confession is made* unto salvation.

God created the mouth and the heart to work as a team. They are the "dynamic duo." Don't try to move into confession with the mouth until you've established belief in the heart. Once you've done both, you're ready to move up to the next rung on the ladder of faith.

⟨ Think about It ⟩

1. Prior to reading this chapter, what did you believe concerning confession? Is the concept of positive confession new to you?

2. Have you confessed the name of the Lord? If so, how? What are some ways you do this in your daily life?

3. What are your thoughts about confessing sins? Do you confess your sins regularly? How do you feel after you confess your sins to God?

4. Write a definition of positive confession as you understand it so far.

5. What must your confession contain to be effective?

6. What would be the result if you began trying positive confession without first going through the other required steps?

7. How did God create the world in Genesis 1?

8. Compare the power of confession with firing a gun. What is the bullet? What is the gunpowder?

9. How do you create a clear image in your heart?

10. What two things must be present for your faith to work?

11. How do you know when you are ready to confess God's Word? Can you give a specific example from your own life?

12. What is God's "dynamic duo"? What happens when the two are in disagreement?

❧ Reflect on It ❧

Whosoever therefore shall confess me before men, him will I confess also before my Father which is in heaven. But whosoever shall deny me before men, him will I also deny before my Father which is in heaven.

—*Matthew 10:32–33*

My prayer in the power of the Word:

_____

_____

_____

_____

_____

I acknowledge my sin unto thee, and mine iniquity have I not hid. I said, I will confess my transgressions unto the LORD; and thou forgavest the iniquity of my sin.

—*Psalm 32:5*

My prayer in the power of the Word:

_____

_____

_____

_____

_____

_____

That if thou shalt confess with thy mouth the Lord Jesus, and shalt believe in thine heart that God hath raised him from the dead, thou shalt be saved. For with the heart man believeth unto righteousness; and with the mouth confession is made unto salvation.

—Romans 10:9–10

My prayer in the power of the Word:

_____

_____

_____

_____

_____

_____

Do It

1. Make a clear and forceful confession of Christ's name. Write a personal profession of faith in your journal. Confess the Lord's name aloud to another individual. (Extra credit for confessing to a stranger!) How might you make a gentle confession of your faith to the supermarket checker or the lady who cuts your hair?

2. Make a point of confessing your sins today. Spend a few extra minutes with your Bible and journal. Begin by praying for the Holy Spirit to reveal to you any hidden areas of sin. Read through Psalm 51:1–12 a couple of times and pray it back to the Lord. Start confessing, and jot down each confession in your journal. Express your repentance and your clear intention to turn away from each of the sins you confessed. Ask God to help you overcome particularly difficult areas of sin. Finish by thanking the Lord for His forgiveness.

3. Engage another Christian in a conversation about the different meanings of confession. Did she have preconceived notions similar to yours? Does she know about or understand positive confession? Does she have any misconceptions that you can help clear up? Let her know what you've been learning and how it is helping you.

4. Read Matthew 17:14–20. Summarize the story in your journal; then write the answers to the following questions: Why weren't the disciples able to cast out the demon? Who gave the disciples the authority to cast out demons in the first place? What does Jesus say about the power of faith? How does this apply to your own positive confession?

5. Review Steps 1 through 5 and determine where you are in the steps. If you've done everything up to and including meditation, continue meditating, and ask God for leading about the timing of your confession. Do you believe in your heart—in every fiber and all the way down to your bones—that you have what you need? When you do, and the timing is right, make your confession!

6. Once you have made your confession, keep repeating it as often as you can. Tell your spouse. Tell your kids. Tell your friends. Write it in big letters in your journal. Pray it several times throughout the day, especially when you wake in the morning and before you fall asleep at night.

Step Seven:
Act on the Word

And why call ye me Lord, Lord, and do not the things which I say?

—*Luke 6:46*

We have discussed the importance of identifying your problem, making a quality decision to overcome it through God's Word, and finding your "title deed" to a solution in the Word. We've also talked about hearing the Word, meditating the Word, and confessing the Word. Once you've taken these vital steps, it's time to go on to the next one: acting on the Word. This is another place where many Christians tend to short-circuit their faith because they haven't seen any results yet. Nobody in the Bible makes a stronger case for acting on your faith than James. Read this familiar passage:

What doth it profit, my brethren, though a man say he hath faith, and have not works? Can faith save him? If a brother or sister be naked, and destitute of daily food, and one of you say unto them, Depart in peace, be ye warmed and filled; notwithstanding ye give them not those things which are needful to the body; what doth it profit? Even so faith, if it hath not works, is dead, being alone. Yea, a man may say, Thou hast faith, and I have works: shew me thy faith without thy works, and I will shew thee my faith by my works. Thou believest that there is one God; thou doest well: the devils also believe, and tremble. But wilt thou know, O vain man, that faith without works is dead? Was not Abraham our father justified by works, when he had offered Isaac his son upon the altar? Seest thou how faith wrought with his works, and by works was faith made perfect? And the scripture was fulfilled which saith, Abraham believed God, and it was imputed unto him for righteousness: and he was called the Friend of God. Ye see then how that by works a man is justified, and not by faith only. Likewise also was not Rahab the harlot justified by works, when she had received the messengers, and had sent them out another way? For as the body without the spirit is dead, so faith without works is dead also.

—James 2:14–26

In no uncertain terms James tells us, "Faith without works is dead." It's one of the most frequently quoted phrases in all of Scripture. And it happens to be true! You can generate faith by hearing the Word of God, establish that faith in your heart by meditating on the Word, even put faith into motion by confessing the Word. But unless you take the additional step of acting on it, there's no life in it to produce the thing you need. A more precise Greek translation of the word "works" in that verse is "an act, deed, thing done."[1] Therefore it is accurate to say that faith without corresponding action is dead.

If you really believe all your needs are met according to God's riches in glory by Christ Jesus, you'll act like it. Likewise, true faith in Jesus as your Healer will produce corresponding actions. Living, moving, producing faith will always be accompanied by corresponding action. It's a principle we see repeated throughout Scripture.

> ❈ *If you really believe all your needs are met according to God's riches in glory by Christ Jesus, you'll act like it.*

FAITH IN ACTION

James gives us several outstanding examples of people who backed up their faith with deeds. One of them is Abraham. You'll remember that he and Sarah were given a miracle baby by God when Abraham was a hundred years old. Later God spoke to him and asked him to take his son, Isaac, and sacrifice him on an altar.

At that time Abraham knew God had promised that through Isaac he would be the father of many nations (see Genesis 17:4). He had meditated on the stars of the sky and the sand of the sea while developing an inner image of all the descendants he would have one day (see Genesis 22:17). He had accepted God's announcement that his very name was Father of a Multitude (see Genesis 17:5 AMP). He had taken every step we've seen so far in God's divine order of faith. So when the time came to put his faith into action, notice what he said:

> And Abraham said unto his young men, Abide ye here with the ass; and I and the lad will go yonder and worship, and come again to you.
>
> —*Genesis 22:5*

Did you see that? "I and the lad will go . . . and come again to you." Abraham did more than talk about his faith in God's promise; he was willing to stake his all on it. And he did.

Abraham was more than just a hearer of the Word. He was a doer. His reward was a miraculous realization of the promises of God. Keep in mind, however, that Abraham had taken all the other steps of faith up to this point. That's the difference between Abraham's experience and a lot of the faith failures you hear so much about.

❋ *[Abraham's] reward was a miraculous realization of the promises of God.*

Many people who are sick hear a little bit about faith, read "With his stripes we are healed" (Isaiah 53:5), and confess it a couple of times. Then they hear they're supposed to act on their faith, so they throw their medicine away. When they almost die, they wonder why that faith stuff didn't work for them.

Is it important to act on the Word? Yes! It's essential. But only after you've laid the foundation by doing the previous six steps we've discussed.

God is blamed for a lot of faith failures by people who simply don't know or bother to operate under His divine order concerning faith. Don't blame God if you ignore His established order of faith and things don't work out the way you want them to work out. For example, nowhere in God's Word does it tell anyone to stop taking his or her medicine. And it's not a sin to go to the doctor. Don't let anyone tell you it is. God is still the Healer, whether healing is facilitated by a medical doctor or worked directly by the Great Physician.

The important point to remember is that once you've laid the groundwork for appropriating a promise from God's Word, it is vital to carry it through by acting as if that promise were already a reality in your life.

Let me give you a practical example. You see in the Word that you are to prosper and have abundance (see Deuteronomy 5:33). You see that you are to be the head and not the tail (see Deuteronomy 28:13), the lender and not the borrower (see Proverbs 22:7). Don't wait until your bank accounts start filling up to begin acting like a prosperous person. Act like one now. You may not have a lot of fancy new clothes, but you can keep the ones you have clean and looking their best. Simply begin thinking like a prosperous person, talking like a prosperous person, and acting like a prosperous person.

Do not wait until you see the abundance to start walking in abundance. People with plenty of money don't worry about money all the time. They don't go around crying to everyone about how they can't pay their bills. Therefore, if you're expecting God's Word to be a reality in your life, neither should you!

❊ *Do not wait until you see the abundance to start walking in abundance.*

Does that mean you should charge up all your credit cards and go into debt in order to look more successful than you really are? Of course not! I'm talking about a change in attitude—an adjustment in lifestyle and outlook. I'm talking about grabbing hold of a promise in God's Word and acting as if it is so while living within the means He has provided for you now.

Don't think for a minute that such a shift in behavior will come easily. Old habits and thinking patterns die hard. Furthermore, when your friends and family see you walking in a reality they can't yet see, some of them may give you a hard time. Ignore them. They won't be laughing when the manifestation of God's promise is apparent for all the world to see.

BELIEVE YOU RECEIVE

This business of acting as if the promise were already manifested is intricately tied to an important principle found in Mark 11:23–24. Let's look at these amazing words of Jesus:

For verily I say unto you, That whosoever shall say unto this mountain, Be thou removed, and be thou cast into the sea; and shall not doubt in his heart, but shall believe that those things which he saith shall come to pass; he shall have whatsoever he saith. Therefore I say unto you, What things soever ye desire, when ye pray, believe that ye receive them, and ye shall have them.

Look at that last line as it is translated in the New International Version: "Therefore I tell you, whatever you ask for in prayer, believe that you have received it, and it will be yours."

"Believe that you have received it." In a sense, that's another way of saying, "It's yours in the spiritual realm, so start acting like it. Then you'll see it in the physical realm!"

When you have a bill due that you can't pay, read, hear, and meditate Philippians 4:19 ("My God shall supply all my needs. . . .") until it's an inner reality. Then go to God in prayer and say, "I believe I receive the money to pay this bill now in the name of Jesus Christ."

If you really did believe you received when you prayed, as Mark 11:24 commands, how will you act when you get up off your knees? You will act as if that bill is paid! You'll think as if it's paid. You'll talk as if it's paid. And you'll rest peacefully at night as if it's paid. Your flesh wants to see the bill paid before it acts as if it's paid, but the Kingdom of God doesn't work that way. We walk by faith, not by sight (see 2 Corinthians 5:7).

Now I want to clarify something with this particular example. When you get off your knees, the Holy Spirit may tell you to go out and apply for a particular job—that may be how God is supplying all your needs and paying that bill.

The Word of God also says in 2 Thessalonians 3:10 that if you don't work you don't eat. Don't expect God to bless you if you are being irresponsible and lazy. But if you are doing all you know to do to follow these steps in God's order of faith in the natural as well as in the Spirit, you can have total confidence that you have what you are confessing.

A change of action must always precede a change of situation, not the other way around. When you're acting on real faith, your outward circumstances will be shaped by your belief and actions.

> ❋ *A change of action must always precede a change of situation.*

Start developing a belief that you are walking in the blessings of God. Cultivate a strong, Word-based conviction that God's favor is upon you and goes before you. Then start acting as if those things are so. It will absolutely turn your life around.

HALFHEARTED OBEDIENCE

Not only does the Bible give us some great examples of people who acted on the Word, it also shows us some who didn't and missed a blessing as a result. For instance, one of the first times the disciples met Jesus, they had an opportunity to act on a word from Him. Look at how they responded:

Now when he [Jesus] had left speaking, he said unto Simon, Launch out into the deep, and let down your nets for a draught [catch]. And Simon answering said unto him, Master, we have toiled all the night, and have taken nothing: nevertheless at thy word I will let down the net.

—*Luke 5:4–5*

Notice the exact wording of Jesus' command: "Let down your nets [plural] for a [catch]." Yet Peter's response was, "I will let down the net [singular]." Peter was probably thinking, *What does this carpenter know about fishing? I'm the expert on fishing here, and I didn't catch anything all night long. But I'll throw out one net just to humor the preacher.* You know the result:

And when they had this done, they inclosed a great multitude of fishes: and their net brake. And they beckoned unto their partners, which were in the other ship, that they should come and help them. And they came, and filled both the ships, so that they began to sink.

—*Luke 5:6–7*

Halfhearted obedience is no obedience at all. Jesus' desire was to bless these men, to provide them with such an enormous catch that they could afford to take an entire year off work and follow Him. That's precisely what would have happened had they acted on His Word and taken every net they owned.

Partial action in faith will yield some results. Total action will yield great results.

❄ *Partial action in faith will yield some results.*
Total action will yield great results.

Another classic biblical example of reluctance to act on the Word is Naaman in the book of 2 Kings. You'll recall that Naaman was a Gentile army general from Syria who was stricken with leprosy, a hideous and incurable disease.

> Now Naaman, captain of the host of the king of Syria, was a great man with his master, and honourable, because by him the LORD had given deliverance unto Syria: he was also a mighty man in valour, but he was a leper.
>
> —*2 Kings 5:1*

Eventually, Naaman heard about a great man of God, Elisha, who might be able to miraculously cure his disease. So he paid Elisha a visit.

> So Naaman came with his horses and with his chariot, and stood at the door of the house of Elisha. (v. 9)

He found Elisha willing to help him, but when Naaman heard the prophet's prescription he took offense:

> And Elisha sent a messenger unto him, saying, Go and wash in Jordan seven times, and thy flesh shall come again to thee, and thou shalt be clean. But Naaman was wroth, and went away, and said, Behold, I thought, He will

surely come out to me, and stand, and call on the name of the LORD his God, and strike his hand over the place, and recover the leper. Are not Abana and Pharpar, rivers of Damascus, better than all the waters of Israel? May I not wash in them, and be clean? So he turned and went away in a rage. (vv. 10–12)

Elisha's response outraged Naaman for several reasons. First, Naaman was an important foreign dignitary and this country preacher didn't even bother to come out and meet him! Second, Naaman expected a miracle worker to come out and do a dance around him or perform some spectacular ceremony. Instead, he was told to go dip himself in the muddy, nasty Jordan River. He walked away angry and just as sick as when he came.

If it hadn't been for some wise encouragement and reasoning from one of his servants, Naaman would have died of that awful disease. Ultimately, he swallowed his pride, acted on the word from God's man, and received his miracle:

And his servants came near, and spake unto him, and said, My father, if the prophet had bid thee do some great thing, wouldest thou not have done it? How much rather then, when he saith to thee, Wash, and be clean? Then went he down, and dipped himself seven times in Jordan, according to the saying of the man of God: and his flesh came again like unto the flesh of a little child, and he was clean. (vv. 13–14)

I see many Christians who act just like Naaman. They have a great need but refuse to walk in simple obedience to God's Word or the instructions of the leaders He has placed them under. Without going through the steps in God's divine order of faith, they want the pastor to personally pray over them. But they are acting like unbelievers. Like Naaman, they don't pray and seek God and His Word for an answer. They simply come to the man or woman of God for a quick and easy "supernatural fix."

When the pastor or minister gives them instructions in the Word or directs them to an anointed staff member or counselor, they take offense. If God's Word or the church leader calls for anything other than what they want to do, they walk away—angry at God, the pastor, and the church.

Simple, childlike obedience to the Word of God and His ministers who are acting according to His Word will never be unproductive or go unrewarded. Simply hear the Word of the Lord and act on it, no matter how foolish or insignificant it may seem. Your faith in God and His Word will be richly rewarded.

> ❋ *Simple, childlike obedience to the Word of God and His ministers . . . will never be unproductive or go unrewarded.*

THE RIGHT FOUNDATION

In Luke 6, Jesus bluntly told a group of listeners, "Don't call Me Lord if you're not going to do what I say."

And why call ye me, Lord, Lord, and do not the things which I say? Whosoever cometh to me, and heareth my sayings, and doeth them, I will shew you to whom he is like: He is like a man which built an house, and digged deep, and laid the foundation on a rock: and when the flood arose, the stream beat vehemently upon that house, and could not shake it: for it was founded upon a rock. But he that heareth, and doeth not, is like a man that without a foundation built an house upon the earth; against which the stream did beat vehemently, and immediately it fell; and the ruin of that house was great.

—*Luke 6:46–49*

If you will purpose to become a person who not only hears God's Word but does it as well, no storm in life will ever shake you. Nothing the Devil throws at you will get the upper hand. Your life will be founded on the immovable rock of obedience to Jesus Christ.

Acting on the Word. It's another crucial step in getting from any problem to God's wonderful answer.

∾ Think about It ∾

1. Read James 2:14–26 again. In your own words, explain what is meant by "faith without works is dead." Use an example from your own life to illustrate your explanation.

2. Why is Abraham a great example of faith in action? What Scriptures back up your answer?

3. Why do many believers fail when they act on their faith?

4. Does acting in faith mean never going to the doctor or taking medicine? If you do seek natural means of healing, does that mean you have no faith in God to heal you?

5. Find several examples in Scripture of believers acting on faith. What was difficult about that action? What was the result?

6. How does the kingdom of God differ from the natural realm when it comes to changing circumstances and beliefs?

7. Give an example of halfhearted obedience. What results do you get with partial faith in action? Total faith in action?

8. In what situations have you thought and behaved like Peter or Naaman? Did you ultimately succeed or fail in receiving from God?

9. Is it true that God helps those who help themselves? Explain your answer.

10. What will never go unrewarded or prove unproductive?

11. What does it mean to say that Jesus is your Lord? How is that the right foundation?

12. What is the ultimate purpose for learning the truths in Scripture?

⌇ Reflect on It ⌇

What doth it profit, my brethren, though a man say he hath faith, and have not works? Can faith save him? If a brother or sister be naked, and destitute of daily food, and one of you say unto them, Depart in peace, be ye warmed and filled; notwithstanding ye give them not those things which are needful to the body; what doth it profit? Even so faith, if it hath not works, is dead, being alone.

—James 2:14–17

My prayer in the power of the Word:

_____

_____

_____

_____

_____

For verily I say unto you, That whosoever shall say unto this mountain, Be thou removed, and be thou cast into the sea; and shall not doubt in his heart, but shall believe that those things which he saith shall come to pass; he shall have whatsoever he saith. Therefore I say unto you, What things soever ye desire, when ye pray, believe that ye receive them, and ye shall have them.

—Mark 11:23–24

My prayer in the power of the Word:

_____

_____

_____

_____

_____

And why call ye me, Lord, Lord, and do not the things which I say? Whosoever cometh to me, and heareth my sayings, and doeth them, I will shew you to whom he is like: He is like a man which built an house, and digged deep, and laid the foundation on a rock: and when the flood arose, the stream beat vehemently upon that house, and could not shake it: for it was founded upon a rock. But he that heareth, and doeth not, is like a man that without a foundation built an house upon the earth; against which the stream did beat vehemently, and immediately it fell; and the ruin of that house was great.

—Luke 6:46–49

My prayer in the power of the Word:

_____

_____

_____

_____

_____

_____

Do It

1. Meditate on Mark 11:23–24 for a day. Continue to meditate on those verses the next day too, and at the end of the day make a list of how this truth changed the way you thought, spoke, and acted.

2. Find a promise in the Bible that you have never really studied, meditated, or acted upon. How must you change your thinking, speaking, and behavior in order to appropriate that promise for your life?

3. Do a word study in your Bible for the word *works.* Copy down each verse you find. What do the verses mean? How will you respond?

4. Identify a person in your life who seems to have it together in an area that you struggle with. Ask if you might talk with that person. Meet with him, and try to gain an understanding of the *beliefs* that underscore his behavior and the *actions* he takes to put those beliefs to work. Make a list in your journal.
Belief:
Action:

5. In your journal, write your confession from Step 6 at the top
    of a page. Now ask yourself, *How does a person who has this con-*
    cern behave? Make a list of everything you can think of. What
    should you do? What should you refrain from doing?

6. Look at your list from the previous question. Which of
    these things can you start doing today? Choose two or
    three or more, and commit to doing them. Make notes
    in your journal about your ideas for *how* you will accom-
    plish these actions.

Step Eight:
Apply the Pressure of Patience

> That ye be not slothful, but followers of them
> who through faith and patience inherit the
> promises.
>
> —*Hebrews 6:12*

Although this book is dedicated to laying out the ten steps of faith that will produce an answer to any problem, you should be aware that you might not always get through all ten steps before your answer appears. Sometimes your faith will produce after doing only the first four or five steps. Other problems may surrender after you've taken the seven steps we've discussed up to this point.

From time to time, however, you'll encounter a situation that requires you to "go the distance." That's when you need to be prepared to take the next step in God's divine order of faith: applying the pressure of patience.

PATIENCE: MORE THAN "PUTTING UP WITH IT"

When most of us hear the word *patience,* we think in terms of "putting up with" or "enduring" something. If you're caught in traffic, you remind yourself to have patience that you'll get there eventually. If your boss assigns you to work with an extremely irritating person for a month, you force a smile and say, "I can deal with it. I'm a patient person." But when the Bible talks about patience, it is referring to something entirely different.

Biblical patience isn't gritting your teeth and bearing some unpleasant or painful burden. In fact, trouble, irritation, pain, and affliction are always from the Devil and should be strenuously resisted by every believer. When Satan tries to put sickness on you, you're not to passively put up with it. It's not from God, so get aggressive and kick it out of your life!

> ❋ *Patience stands on the Word of God—no matter what.*

When God's Word mentions patience, it's talking about the ability to remain constant. A person with biblical patience remains fixed and immovable regardless of how the surrounding circumstances look or feel. Patience stands on the Word of God—no matter what—and aggressively applies pressure to the problem. This is the very quality James talks about in the following familiar passage of Scripture:

My brethren, count it all joy when ye fall into divers temptations; knowing this, that the trying of your faith worketh patience. But let patience have her perfect work, that ye may be perfect and entire, wanting nothing.

—James 1:2–4

A lot of Christians misunderstand what these verses are saying. When James says, "The trying of your faith worketh patience," he's not suggesting that patience is produced or created as a result of the trial, as many people believe. Rather, he is saying, "Trouble puts patience to work!"

Why is that a cause for joy? Because patience enables you to overcome trouble, to put pressure on the Enemy and the problem, causing the situation and circumstances to line up with God's Word. That's why the joy of the Lord is your strength (see Nehemiah 8:10)! It slams the Enemy with God's Word.

If you're in the midst of a trial, you want the power of patience and joy, not bitterness, working in you. Bitterness has no power to help you. You don't want to employ grief, despair, anger, or guilt either. These emotions and thoughts might be a natural response to the trial, but your focus should not remain there.

Rejoice when you face a trial because it puts the power of patience to work on your behalf! That truth is echoed in Romans 5:3–4:

But we glory in tribulations also: knowing that tribulation worketh [employs] patience; and patience, experience; and experience, hope.

❈ *Rejoice when you face a trial because it puts the power of patience to work on your behalf!*

That's why James told us to rejoice when patience is about to come on the scene. Patience hires experience, experience hires hope, and hope is a powerful thing. It ranks right up there with faith and love (see 1 Corinthians 13:13). In fact, it was David's experience and hope that gave him the confidence to face the giant, Goliath. He said, "Thy servant slew both the lion and the bear: and this uncircumcised Philistine shall be as one of them, seeing he hath defied the armies of the living God" (1 Samuel 17:36).

However, as James points out, it all begins with patience—patience employed for the testing of your faith. Notice what James says next:

But let patience have her perfect work, that ye may be perfect and entire, wanting nothing.

—*James 1:4*

Note that the Word says, "Let patience. . . ." That suggests that you have the ability to either permit or prevent patience from performing her perfect work on your behalf. What is her perfect work? "That ye may be perfect [complete] and entire, wanting [lacking] nothing."

DOUBLE-MINDED OR SINGLE-PURPOSED

We just saw in James 1:4 that patience, if allowed to do its work, can put you in a place where you have everything you need. But you may be asking, "How do I *let* patience work? Do I just sit around and wait for it to happen?"

Not a chance. The very next verses give us some insight into what it takes to put patience to work for you:

> If any of you lack wisdom, let him ask of God, that giveth to all men liberally, and upbraideth not; and it shall be given him. But let him ask in faith, nothing wavering. For he that wavereth is like a wave of the sea driven with the wind and tossed.
>
> —*James 1:5–6*

Obviously, when it comes to dealing successfully with trials or troubles, the wisdom of God can be a very precious commodity. As the book of Proverbs indicates again and again, wisdom brings success, prosperity, long life, and the knowledge of what to do in any situation.

> ❋ *Wisdom brings success, prosperity, long life, and the knowledge of what to do in any situation.*

So what does this verse tell you to do in order to get wisdom? Simply ask in faith. That shouldn't come as a surprise. Everything in the Christian life comes back to faith. In fact, the next verse delivers a pretty blunt warning for the Christian who doesn't have time for "that faith stuff":

> For let not that man think that he shall receive any thing of the Lord. A double minded man is unstable in all his ways.
>
> —*James 1:7–8*

When you ask God for something, ask in faith. If you don't, you're fooling yourself. God is not going to move on your behalf if you do not have faith in Him to move on your behalf. "Without faith it is impossible to please [God]" (Hebrews 11:6).

How do you ask in faith? It's not that hard! Ask Him according to His Word. Here is how I do it. I pray,

Father, in the name of Jesus, I need wisdom. According to Your Word in James, chapter 1, You said if any man lacks wisdom let him ask, and You will give it liberally and upbraid not. Lord, I ask in faith right now for Your wisdom in this matter. I believe I receive what I've asked for according to Your Word. Philippians 4:19 says that You shall supply all my needs according to Your riches in glory by Christ Jesus. And in Colossians 2:2–3 You said that in Jesus are hid all the treasures of wisdom and knowledge. Therefore I have wisdom and all my needs are taken care of. I know that You've heard me, and I know I have the petition that I have asked. In the name of Jesus that settles it, and I praise You and thank You for Your love toward me. Amen.

Then I get up off my knees and go forward, knowing and acting as if I have received. That's asking in faith.

If, on the other hand, I ask timidly and full of doubt, James says I am like a wave of the sea being blown every which way. The wavering believer says, "I am healed. . . . No, I think I'm sick. . . . No, I'm healed. . . . Wait a minute, I think I'm sick." Don't expect anything from heaven if you pray like that!

"A double minded man is unstable in all his ways." Double-mindedness, in a sense, is the opposite of patience. You'll remember we defined patience as being mentally fixed and immovable, which puts pressure on the problem. When you are double-minded, you're being moved in whichever direction the winds of adversity happen to be blowing. All the pressure is on you!

When trouble comes, the battleground of patience truly is the mind, which is part of the "soulish" realm (mind, will, and emotions). Look at what Jesus said to do when encountering tribulation:

In your patience possess ye your souls.

—Luke 21:19

The mind is the arena of faith. If patience is going to be allowed to do its work, there has to be a capturing or arresting of the soulish realm. It is hard to pray in faith if your mind is reeling with thoughts of doubt and unbelief.

Have you ever tried to pray and found it impossible because the traffic in your mind was so noisy? At those times, stay with it. Patience will enable you to possess your soul and help you to quiet your mind. Then, and only then, are you in a position to be single-minded, to come into agreement with God's Word, and to pray in faith.

❋ *Patience will enable you to possess your soul and help you to quiet your mind.*

FAITH'S POTENT PARTNER

Inheriting the promises in God's Word is the bottom line to everything you're reading in this book. These steps represent the God-ordained progression for seeing God's glorious promises become a reality in your life. And according to Hebrews 6:12, two spiritual forces work in tandem to make that happen:

That ye be not slothful, but followers of them who through faith and patience inherit the promises.

"Faith and patience." My friend and father in the faith, Kenneth Copeland, calls them "the power twins."[1] As this Scripture indicates, they work together to bring God's great and precious promises to pass in your life.

Faith without patience is one-legged. The two must be joined together to be truly effective. We see this vital connection echoed in Hebrews 10 as well:

Cast not away therefore your confidence, which hath great recompence of reward. *For ye have need of patience,* that, after ye have done the will of God, ye might receive the promise. For yet a little while, and he that shall come will come, and will not tarry. *Now the just shall live by faith:* but if any man draw back, my soul shall have no pleasure in him.

—*Hebrews 10:35–38, emphasis mine*

Many believers cast away their confidence right before their miracle is about to be manifested, simply because they lack patience. This is a tragedy that I want you to avoid!

If you're standing on the Word for your healing, Satan is going to intensify the symptoms in order to get you to throw your confidence away. Unless patience is standing behind your faith and trust in God, putting pressure on the problem, you're likely to give up and decide it's not working—often right before your faith in God and His Word is about to produce a breakthrough for you.

What is God's prescription for not throwing away your confidence on the brink of a miracle? "You have need of patience!" Patience partners with faith to keep pressure on the Devil until he turns loose and runs for the hills. Patience undergirds your faith, and without faith it is impossible to please God. That's why patience is an essential step on the road to your miraculous victory.

∽ Think about It ∽

1. Before reading this chapter, what was your idea of patience?

2. What should be your attitude toward trials, temptations, pain, and affliction? Are those things from God? Should you submit to them?

3. What is the biblical definition of *patience*? What does James 1:2–4 say puts patience to work? Why is that a cause for joy?

4. How do you develop patience? Does it just happen automatically as you get older?

5. What attitude should you have along with patience? Why?

6. What do you need when you are facing a trial? How do you get it?

7. What is the difference between "suffering" in the typical sense, and "longsuffering" in the biblical sense?

8. Just how important is faith in the believer's life? Cite Scripture to back up your answer.

9. What does it mean to "let patience have her perfect work" (James 1:4)?

10. Explain the difference between *patience* and *double-mindedness*. Where is the battle between these two fought? How is the battle won?

11. What areas of your life demand the most patience? How can you exercise new levels of patience when those circumstances arise?

12. How does patience play a part in (1) inheriting the promises of God; (2) staying confident in the Lord; (3) defeating the Devil; and (4) pleasing God?

⬯ Reflect on It ⬯

My brethren, count it all joy when ye fall into divers temptations; knowing this, that the trying of your faith worketh patience. But let patience have her perfect work, that ye may be perfect and entire, wanting nothing.

—James 1:2–4

My prayer in the power of the Word:

_____

_____

_____

_____

_____

But we glory in tribulations also: knowing that tribulation worketh patience; and patience, experience; and experience, hope: And hope maketh not ashamed; because the love of God is shed abroad in our hearts by the Holy Ghost which is given unto us.

—Romans 5:3–5

My prayer in the power of the Word:

_____

_____

_____

_____

_____

If any of you lack wisdom, let him ask of God, that giveth to all men liberally, and upbraideth not; and it shall be given him. But let him ask in faith, nothing wavering. For he that wavereth is like a wave of the sea driven with the wind and tossed.

—James 1:5–6

My prayer in the power of the Word:

_____

_____

_____

_____

_____

Do It

1. Look up the words *patience, perseverance,* and *longsuffering* in your Bible or concordance. What do you learn about the importance of these attributes? How can you develop them? Why are they necessary? What are their rewards? Write your thoughts in your journal.

2. Talk to a member of your family or someone who knows you well. Ask him about your patience. Does he consider you to be a patient person? In what situations do you seem patient, and what situations tend to try your patience? What does this tell you about how fruitful your Christian walk is so far?

3. Examine how you typically practice patience. Is it with joy? Or is it with barely suppressed resentment and anxiety? Write down some ideas for incorporating joyfulness into your exercise of patience.

4. Take some time to specifically ask the Lord for wisdom. Talk to Him about the problem you are facing, and lay out any difficulties you're having with patience. Base your prayer on specific verses you've found in Scripture. Then get up from your prayer believing you have received the wisdom you've asked for.

5. Practice thinking of patience in terms of remaining constant, fixed, and immovable, standing on the Word of God. The next time you are irritated and find yourself thinking, *I just have to be patient,* shift your thought pattern. Say to yourself, *It doesn't matter what's happening here. I am standing firm on the Word of God. I don't have to muster up patience—I already have it in the name of Jesus! Patience will work for me. My circumstances do not determine my attitude. My eyes are fixed on Jesus no matter what!* Do this as often as you need to throughout your day. If you're standing in a long line at the bank or sitting in traffic or dealing with your testy two-year-old, see if your new knowledge about patience changes your attitude.

6. Think about a problem you've been dealing with. What did you confess about the results you expect (Step 6)? In what ways have you been acting on the Word (Step 7)? Now, what will be required for you to apply the pressure of patience? Do you simply need to wait? Is there any decisive action you must take in order to successfully exercise patience? If so, make sure you put that into effect immediately.

Step Nine:
Wait for God's Timing

Therefore I will look unto the LORD; I will
wait for the God of my salvation: my God will
hear me.

—*Micah 7:7*

Each step we've looked at thus far in God's divine order
of faith has been closely linked to the step that preceded it. The
ninth step is no exception. It uses the previous step, "Apply the
pressure of patience," as a springboard to wait for God's timing.

I can almost hear you groaning, "Oh, no. Not another 'wait
on the Lord' lecture." I don't know what you've been taught in
the past, but this is good news! I guarantee you're going to like
it because it is one more weapon in your arsenal to get victory
over every problem you face.

A TIME AND A SEASON

One of the most important truths you can ever grasp in your
Christian life is this: with God, there is an appointed time and

a due season for everything. That's the theme of this beautiful passage of Scripture from one of the wisest men who ever lived:

> To every thing there is a season, and a time to every purpose under the heaven: A time to be born, and a time to die; a time to plant, and a time to pluck up that which is planted; a time to kill, and a time to heal; a time to break down, and a time to build up; a time to weep, and a time to laugh; a time to mourn, and a time to dance; a time to cast away stones, and a time to gather stones together; a time to embrace, and a time to refrain from embracing; a time to get, and a time to lose; a time to keep, and a time to cast away; a time to rend, and a time to sew; a time to keep silence, and a time to speak; a time to love, and a time to hate; a time of war, and a time of peace.
>
> —*Ecclesiastes 3:1–8*

God has an established season of time for every purpose in your life. He sees the end from the beginning and has a master time sheet with ordered seasons for all things to take place. This is a concept you must keep in mind as you begin to pray and believe for certain things in your life.

❋ God has an established season of time for every purpose in your life.

Why is God's timing so important? First of all, He knows what you can handle and when you can handle it, so you want your life to be guided by Him. And second, the things for which you're asking will directly and indirectly affect other people, believers and unbelievers. Our lives are linked in a complex, interconnected web, and only our heavenly Father sits above it all, working all things together for our good (see Romans 8:28).

We serve a God who is not limited by our concepts of time and distance. That's a lesson He brought home to me very clearly when I was a young believer. As a very small boy, I asked why God didn't have a father. I had a father. My father had a father. Everyone in the world had a father as far as I knew. Who then, I wondered, was God's father? I never got a satisfactory answer from anyone I asked.

Years later, when I began to mature in the Word and develop a relationship with God, I asked Him myself. One day while praying, I just asked point-blank, "God, who is Your daddy?" I'll never forget His response.

"Son, I created the system you are trying to put Me in. I created the system of reproduction, in which everything produces after its own kind. I stand outside that system because it came out of me. I AM that I AM, the beginning and the end. I have always been here. You can't put Me in time, because time came out of Me. Don't put Me in anything I created."

"Yes sir, Boss," was my quick reply. But I've never forgotten that truth. I frequently see Christians who need to get that understanding. They have God on their personal timetable. If He doesn't come through when they think He should, they assume something must be wrong. They need to understand God has a time and purpose for everything under heaven.

You may be wondering about some things today. You may be saying, "Lord, when is my business going to take off?" There is a due season. "Where is the anointing and power to minister I've been praying for?" There is a due season. "Where is the spouse I desire so greatly?" Child of God, there is a due season. Your time is coming.

The key to avoiding frustration, fear, and the temptation to quit when standing in faith on God's Word is understanding there is a time and due season for everything.

YOUR DUE SEASON

As a pastor who has counseled hundreds of believers, I regularly meet with people who are impatient and frustrated with trying to appropriate the promises of God. Invariably, as I talk with them I am reminded of Galatians 6:7–9 (emphasis mine):

> Be not deceived; God is not mocked: for whatsoever a man soweth, that shall he also reap. For he that soweth to his flesh shall of the flesh reap corruption; but he that soweth to the Spirit shall of the Spirit reap life everlasting. *And let us not be weary in well doing: for in due season we shall reap, if we faint not.*

This passage is loaded with truth for the believer trying to get from the problem to the answer. First, we're reminded of the universal law of sowing and reaping. Obviously, this refers to more than just literal seeds. We sow many things in the natural course of daily living: money, words, attitudes, time, deeds. All of these, good or bad, are seeds we sow.

Whatever you are right now is the result of what you have sowed in the past. That's difficult for a lot of people to accept. It's much more comfortable to blame others or the Devil for all their problems. The fact is, the Devil really can't do anything to you until you give him an opening.

> ❈ *The fact is, the Devil really can't do anything to you until you give him an opening.*

I found it to be very liberating when I finally faced the fact that my circumstances today are a product of the kind of seed I sowed yesterday. It gave me hope that if the choices I had made in the past brought me to where I was now, then the choices I made now could take me where I knew God wanted me to go in the future.

When it comes to dealing with the frustration so many believers feel concerning the things of faith, it's the last verse in that passage that we really need to consider:

And let us not be weary in well doing: for in due season we shall reap, if we faint not. (v. 9)

This is so important! And it is precisely where many believers miss the mark. Somewhere along the road to their answer, the persecution, the affliction, or the seeming lack of results causes them to grow weary. It has happened to the most seasoned faith warriors.

Does this apply to you too? You are going strong—reading and meditating God's Word, speaking the truth of God's promises, going where you're supposed to go, praying, fasting, and doing anything else you can think of to do—when suddenly you sit down and realize you're tired. That is the critical moment when you are most tempted to move off of your stand of faith and quit. So that is the time you need to remember to "not be weary in well doing." Why? Because you'll reap in due season if you'll just hang on.

✳ *You'll reap in due season if you'll just hang on.*

Don't get tired of doing, speaking, and living God's Word. Don't get tired of standing for your healing. Don't get tired of tithing and giving. Stay in the Word. Your due season of harvest and blessing is coming. God has appointed it!

NO CAVE-INS

"In due season we shall reap, if we faint not." Where the promises of God are concerned, it's not a matter of *if* He's going to come through; it's a matter only of *when*. His Word assures you of that, but God only knows how many times you've quit just before your due season arrived.

The Word also tells you what stops you from reaching your due season: fainting. That word *faint* means "to grow weak, lose spirit or courage."[1] If you don't cave in under the pressure of circumstances and mocking voices, you will reap. So don't stop! Your answer is on its way.

"But I'm not seeing any progress!" What we often don't realize is that progress is being made in the spiritual realm—and we simply can't see until it suddenly breaks forth. A lot can be happening beneath the surface that you never perceive. Therefore, you cannot go by only what you can see.

Don't quit just because your mountain doesn't seem to be moving. It could be breaking loose like crazy right below the surface. You may be only moments away from seeing it fly up and fall into the sea (see Mark 11:23–24). Avoid fainting and you're home free!

Where does fainting start? Hebrews 12:3 (emphasis mine) tells us that fainting begins in your mind:

> For consider him that endured such contradiction of sinners against himself, *lest ye be wearied and faint in your minds.*

If you're going to get weary and faint, thereby failing to receive your due season of harvest, it will start in your mind—the battleground of faith. The mind is where Satan attacks you, and his most common method is to come with suggestions. "It's not working. God doesn't care about you. You're not worthy," he'll whisper. His aim is to get you to "faint in your mind."

How do you defeat this onslaught of the Enemy? Follow Jesus' example and defeat him with "It is written." Remind the Enemy and yourself of Galatians 6:9. Meditate on it and other verses of Scripture that will build your faith and give you strength to keep pressing on to what God has for you. Always remember that if you just keep believing, speaking, and acting on God's Word, the time must come when you will reap your harvest.

❋ If you just keep believing, speaking, and acting on God's Word, the time must come when you will reap your harvest.

TRUST GOD'S TIMING

Another pitfall many believers fall into when waiting on the promises of God is comparing their experiences to those of other believers. I remember when people used to constantly ask me when I was going to go on television with this ministry. My reply was always, "It is not my time."

Others would ask, "When are you going to write a book?"

Again, my consistent answer was, "It is not my time."

Then one day the Lord said, "It's your time," and I immediately started receiving instructions from the Holy Spirit about what to do and how to do it.

Perhaps God has placed some things in your heart, yet you're not presently seeing any opportunity to fulfill them. Hang on. If you'll stay in faith, the day will come when you'll hear the Holy Spirit say, "It's time."

❋ If you'll stay in faith, the day will come when you'll hear the Holy Spirit say, "It's time."

Keep in mind too that it is important not to operate in jealousy or envy when you see God moving in the lives of others. Learn how to rejoice with those who rejoice, because your time is coming. When you see God moving miraculously in another's life, it's easy to sit back and grumble, "Why him and not me?" That's pure poison! It will kill the good work God is trying to bring about in you.

Develop a childlike trust in God's timing. He loves you and has your best interests in mind. And when you see someone else's due season arrive, rejoice for him or her and receive hope that your due season is on its way.

HURRY UP AND WAIT

One of the hardest things for Christians to do is to wait for God's perfect timing after He's placed a burning vision of something in their spirit. Once God has shown them what He wants, the tendency is to run out ahead of God and mess things up. Don't do that! If God has given you a vision—it may be a ministry, a spouse, a job, or something else—learn to wait on God's due season.

> And the LORD answered me, and said, Write the vision, and make it plain upon tables, that he may run that readeth it. For the vision is yet for an appointed time, but at the end it shall speak, and not lie: though it tarry, wait for it; because it will surely come, it will not tarry.
>
> —*Habakkuk 2:2–3*

Here is my advice for any believer with a vision from God: first, write it down plainly. That way you can examine it clearly and not get carried off into something God didn't really show you. Then when you start feeling impatient or weary, remember, "The vision is yet for an appointed time . . . though it tarry, wait for it; because it will surely come."

If your vision seems to be "tarrying," don't lose heart. Wait—it will surely come in due season. You have God's Word on it.

"But I don't know how much longer I can wait. I'm really getting tired of standing!"

That's okay. Keep standing. God has made provision for you:

Hast thou not known? Hast thou not heard, that the everlasting God, the LORD, the Creator of the ends of the earth, fainteth not, neither is weary? There is no searching of his understanding. He giveth power to the faint; and to them that have no might he increaseth strength. Even the youths shall faint and be weary, and the young men shall utterly fall: But they that wait upon the Lord shall renew their strength; they shall mount up with wings as eagles; they shall run, and not be weary; and they shall walk, and not faint.

—*Isaiah 40:28–31*

A GUARANTEED PRESCRIPTION

To wait on the Lord means to serve Him with praise, worship, and adoration as a waiter in a restaurant would serve a customer. If the waiter does an exceptional job of serving, the customer will be motivated to leave a tip.

Child of God, I believe that when we serve God with praise and worship, He is motivated to tip us generously by causing the unrealities of our lives—that which we are believing Him and His Word for—to become realities.

If you are in need of healing, wait on the Lord. If you are in need of a miracle, wait on the Lord. If you've grown weary from standing, wait on the Lord. If you are in need of strength, wait on the Lord. If you're feeling faint, wait on the Lord. It's a guaranteed prescription for gaining the reality of God's Word and being renewed in His strength.

Waiting on the Lord and His timing is the vital ninth step in God's divine order of faith.

◦ Think about It ◦

1. How are all the steps in God's divine order of faith related?

2. Is God ever subject to your timetable?

3. What is God's answer to the question, "Who is Your daddy?" What verses of Scripture support this explanation?

4. What do you avoid when you understand God's timing and wait patiently for it?

5. In light of Galatians 6:7–9, who is responsible for who you are and where you are today?

6. What is the most critical moment in waiting for God's timing?

7. When you feel like fainting, what aren't you seeing?

8. When was the last time you felt faint? How can you defeat that the next time it comes up?

9. Have you ever stepped out of God's timing simply because you wanted to be like someone else or because of peer pressure? What were the results?

10. What do you need to develop to avoid stepping out too soon or too late?

11. What instruction do you find concerning the Lord's vision in Habakkuk 2:2-3?

12. What does it really mean to "wait" upon the Lord?

꧂ Reflect on It ꧂

Therefore I will look unto the LORD; I will wait for the God of my salvation: my God will hear me.

—Micah 7:7

My prayer in the power of the Word:

_____

_____

_____

_____

_____

Be not deceived; God is not mocked: for whatsoever a man soweth, that shall he also reap. For he that soweth to his flesh shall of the flesh reap corruption; but he that soweth to the Spirit shall of the Spirit reap life everlasting. And let us not be weary in well doing: for in due season we shall reap, if we faint not.

—Galatians 6:7–9

My prayer in the power of the Word:

_____

_____

_____

_____

_____

And the LORD answered me, and said, Write the vision, and
make it plain upon tables, that he may run that readeth it.
For the vision is yet for an appointed time, but at the end it
shall speak, and not lie: though it tarry, wait for it; because
it will surely come, it will not tarry.

—*Habakkuk 2:2–3*

My prayer in the power of the Word:

_____

_____

_____

_____

_____

Do It

1. Read Psalm 71. If you can, read it in several translations in order to better understand it. How does this psalm speak to your situation? What does it say to you about your process of waiting? Choose one or more verses from this psalm, copy them down, and meditate on them for the next few days.

2. Has God given you a vision for the fulfillment of His promise to you? Write down the vision in your journal. Make sure it is clear and simple. If you like, copy it down on a separate piece of paper and put it next to your bed or on your wall so you can see it often. Refer back to it whenever you start to feel anxious in your waiting period. Be assured that though the vision may tarry, it will arrive at the appointed time!

3. If you are in a period of waiting and you find yourself impatient for the answer to your prayer to arrive, begin thinking about the purposes God may have for this interim period. Ask God to help you understand what He wants you to learn from this time. Write the following questions in your journal and answer them as best you can, spending as much time as you need, even if it takes a few days:

    • What do I think I'm ready to handle right now?

    • Why do I think I need this blessing I am asking for?

- What are some possible reasons God might not think I'm ready?

- Who else could possibly be affected by the answer to my prayer?

- What does God want me to learn from this waiting period?

When you are finished, think about your answers and how they might help you endure this waiting period with hope and joy as opposed to anxiety.

4. If you are in the midst of a prolonged time of waiting, this is a great time to find ways to serve others, taking the focus off yourself. First, think about the areas of ministry in which you might be interested. A great place to start is your local church, which provides opportunities to serve church members and the community. You could also find out where volunteer opportunities exist in your community. Make a commitment *today* to spend at least one hour a week in service to others.

5. Another way to find comfort during your time of waiting is to comfort someone else. Is there anyone among your friends or acquaintances who could use some TLC? Perhaps you are aware of a person who has recently lost a loved one or endured some other kind of trauma. Maybe you know someone who is gravely ill or in the hospital

or recovering from surgery. Now is the time to reach out! Don't feel you need any special skills, and don't give in to the pressure to "say the right thing." You need only to offer the comfort of your presence, letting that person know you care. Allow God to work through you as He comforts that person through your presence. And be open to further opportunities to meet the person's physical, emotional, and spiritual needs.

6. In this chapter we talked about the necessity of not giving up. If you were to grow weary and give up on waiting for God's answer, what would that look like for you? Write your answer in your journal. Now pray over that, and ask God to keep you strong and help you avoid giving in to weariness. Make a commitment to wait on the Lord no matter what temptations may assault you.

Step Ten:
Expect the Answer

> For surely there is an end; and thine expectation
> shall not be cut off.
>
> —*Proverbs 23:18*

We've now come to the final step in God's established order for getting from any challenge or crisis to a miraculous solution. It is the icing on the cake—the last nail in the Devil's coffin. This important tenth step involves cultivating expectation.

Expectation is a very powerful thing. For better or for worse, it colors your outlook, shapes your attitudes, and influences your actions. Learning to harness its power can make a huge difference in your quality of life.

EXPECTATION DEFINED

To expect means "to anticipate or look forward to the coming or occurrence of . . . to consider probably or certain."[1] When you "expect" something, you start mentally or visually "looking" for its appearance. For example, when your aunt says, "I'm frying chicken tonight. Come on over and have dinner with us," you expect to eat fried chicken when you get there. You are looking for it to be on the table when you arrive. If you show up only to find meatloaf on the table, you're shocked. Why? Because you expected fried chicken.

Expectation not only involves vision (looking for something), but it also involves a change of posture (preparing for something). When you expect something, you begin to suitably position yourself to receive it. Let me illustrate.

When a woman is with child, we say she is what? Expecting. What is she expecting? A baby! And that expectation triggers a lot of preparation. Furniture is purchased. A nursery is decorated. A hospital is chosen, and financial arrangements are made. Every part of that household begins to realign itself in anticipation of the expected arrival.

Now let's say you asked a woman who was going to deliver twins in a month if she was getting ready for the arrival of the babies, and she answered, "No, we're not making any preparations." You'd be dumbfounded. Why? Because expectation implies preparation.

As we're about to see, this is especially true of spiritual expectation. If you truly expect God to do some things in your life, you will do some realigning and preparing. I liken it to the exchange between a pitcher and a catcher in baseball. You'll never see a good catcher stand nonchalantly behind the plate waiting for the next pitch. No, when he's ready to receive, he'll crouch down, get a stable base with his legs, hold up his catcher's mitt, and look right at the pitcher in intense anticipation of the next pitch.

> *If you truly expect God to do some things in your life, you will do some realigning and preparing.*

That is also how the pitcher knows the catcher's ready to receive. He has put himself in the receiving posture. The pitcher is not about to throw the ball until he sees that posture, that the catcher is ready to receive the pitch.

The same is true of God. His heartfelt desire is to throw blessings to you. He's ready to wind up and let healing, prosperity, and deliverance fly; but He can't until you get into a receiving posture—the posture of expectation.

I've spoken with many Christians who are hoping and praying for miracles, yet their posture says they're not ready to receive those miracles. There is no preparation or realignment going on in their lives. Why? Because they don't really expect an answer. They lack genuine expectation.

FOCUSING YOUR EXPECTATION

The Bible has a lot to say about expectation. Let's look as Psalm 62:5–6 for starters:

> My soul, wait thou only upon God; for my expectation is from him. He only is my rock and my salvation: he is my defence; I shall not be moved.

Notice the focus of the psalmist's expectation: "My expectation is from him [God]." That highlights one of the biggest problems Christians have in the area of expectation: improper focus.

Some believers talk a good, religious talk, but when it comes right down to it their expectation is not directed toward God. Some are expecting the world and the world's system to deliver the things that make for happiness. Others expect a relationship to meet their needs. Still others look to their pastor to spoon-feed them and do all their praying for them.

In each case, the person's expectation is focused on something or someone other than God. Yet the psalmist said, "My soul, wait thou only upon God." He's commanding his soul (his mind, will, and emotions) to get its focus off of anything but God.

Properly focused expectation says, "I'm not looking for help from any source but God. If I'm going to have it, it's going to come from Him. If it doesn't come from Him, I don't need it."

THE HOPE CONNECTION

Real Bible expectation often travels with a companion. Her name is "Hope." You see them hanging out together in Philippians 1:20:

> According to my earnest expectation and my hope, that in nothing I shall be ashamed, but that with all boldness, as always, so now also Christ shall be magnified in my body, whether it be by life, or by death.

Hope and earnest expectation complement each other perfectly. They also tend to intensify each other. Hope increases your level of expectation, and expectation raises your level of hope. Here's how.

> ❋ *Hope and earnest expectation . . . tend to intensify each other.*

Let's say you have a bill you just don't have the money to pay. Because you have heard several testimonies of people whose bills have been miraculously paid, you have a little hope that God will meet your need as well. So, you pray and ask God to take care of your bill.

At that point you have a little bit of hope and a fairly low level of expectation. But as you stand on God's Word and meditate the appropriate Scriptures, your need is miraculously met. Now, the next time you are faced with a bill you can't pay, you remember God's faithfulness. You are going to have a larger measure of hope and a higher level of expectation because your faith and trust in Him have grown. This cycle repeats itself each time you experience the faithfulness of God toward His Word. It's an upward spiral of ever-increasing hope and expectancy in Him.

This works in the negative too. If you throw up a halfhearted prayer and never open your Bible, you're not connecting with God and are probably not going to see an answer to your prayer. When nothing happens, you'll say, "Just as I expected. Faith didn't work for me." As a result of your not following God's divine order of faith, over time you develop a negative expectation and are locked in hopelessness.

Just as your expectation is always locked on God, so is your hope. Always remember that your hope is in Him and His Word. When you hope in God, you can expect Him to come through; and when you expect Him to come through, He is your only hope. Hope and expectation work together when your focus is on God.

CULTIVATING EXPECTATION

If you really want to receive everything God so greatly desires to give you, you must begin to cultivate expectancy. A number of biblical examples illustrate how important expectations are when it comes to receiving a miracle.

Remember the four men who lowered the lame man to Jesus through a hole in the ceiling in Luke 5:17? Do you recall the first thing Jesus said to the man?

> And when he saw their faith, he said unto him, Man, thy sins are forgiven thee.
>
> —*Luke 5:20*

This man needed healing, yet Jesus told him his sins were forgiven. Why? Jesus knew that if the man was going to receive his healing, he needed to increase his expectancy. And as we have seen, that requires a change of posture.

The man apparently had a sinful past and as a result didn't feel worthy to be healed by Jesus. Before the man would receive, Jesus had to change his expectation, and that meant dealing with his sense of sinfulness.

A high level of expectancy is almost always a prerequisite for a miracle. The good news is that Jesus—as He did with the man in this passage—is always looking for a way to help us raise our level of expectation.

> ❋ *A high level of expectancy is almost always a prerequisite for a miracle.*

When a crippled man in Jerusalem needed that kind of help one day, the Holy Spirit showed Peter how to give it to him:

> Now Peter and John went up together into the temple at the hour of prayer, being the ninth hour. And a certain man lame from his mother's womb was carried, whom they laid daily at the gate of the temple which is called Beautiful.
>
> —*Acts 3:1–2*

Here was a man who had been crippled all his life. Begging was all he'd ever known. He certainly had no reason to expect to ever walk or work. Apparently, the man kept his eyes on the ground in humility and shame as he begged for alms.

Peter, sensing the man needed a change in posture in order to receive, gave him a command:

And Peter, fastening his eyes upon him with John, said, Look on us. And he gave heed unto them, expecting to receive something of them.

—*Acts 3:4–5*

Peter's demand obviously had its intended effect. The man looked up at them in anticipation of receiving money. He now had expectation, but the wrong one. So Peter raised the man's expectation to another notch:

Then Peter said, Silver and gold have I none; but such as I have give I thee: In the name of Jesus Christ of Nazareth rise up and walk. And he took him by the right hand, and lifted him up.

—*Acts 3:6–7*

Peter said, "Don't expect money. Expect healing." And to help him change his receiving posture even further, Peter grabbed the man by the hand and pulled him to his feet. The result?

And immediately his feet and ankle bones received strength. And he leaping up stood, and walked, and entered with them into the temple, walking, and leaping, and praising God.

—*Acts 3:7–8*

Child of God, I can't overemphasize the importance of earnest expectation in receiving the provision of God. It can turn your road to a miracle from a treacherous mountain trail into a four-lane highway. Expectation places you before the face of God, and He blesses expectant people—those who are looking to Him and Him alone for all their needs to be met.

> ❋ *Expectation places you before the face of God, and He blesses expectant people.*

Cultivate expectancy in every area of your life. Don't just throw your tithe into the church's offering plate and forget about it. Spend the rest of the week in earnest expectation of the windows of heaven opening up and pouring out a blessing. Expect to receive a hundredfold return on all your giving. Expect to walk in health and to be healed when you don't. Expect to be promoted. Expect to have a good marriage. In other words, simply put your faith and trust in God!

Expect *all* the blessings of God to be yours in fullness here and now. It's what He wants for you. He says so in His Word:

For I know the thoughts that I think toward you, saith the LORD, thoughts of peace, and not of evil, to give you an expected end.

—*Jeremiah 29:11*

God desires for you to have peace, prosperity, and an expected end. Don't let go of your earnest expectation—it will come in the end. When you pray according to God's Word, expect an answer!

Expectation is the tenth and final step in God's divine order of faith because expectation is the aspect of faith that says, "I know God is faithful to watch over His Word to perform it!"

Think about It

1. What does expectation do in your life?

2. What do you do when you expect something?

3. How does expectation affect your vision? Your behavior?

4. What is the biggest problem believers have in the area of expectation?

5. Give a negative example and a positive example of how hope and expectation have worked together in your life.

6. How did Peter cultivate the right expectation in the crippled man at the gate called Beautiful (see Acts 3)?

7. Why did Jesus tell the paralytic his sins were forgiven before healing him (see Luke 5)?

8. What are some ways you can make preparation for receiving your miracle?

9. On whom or what should your expectation be focused?

10. How are expectation and hope connected?

11. How do you "expect" in the active rather than the passive sense?

12. How can you cultivate expectancy?

❧ Reflect on It ❧

My soul, wait thou only upon God; for my expectation is from him. He only is my rock and my salvation: he is my defence; I shall not be moved.

—Psalm 62:5–6

My prayer in the power of the Word:

_____

_____

_____

_____

_____

According to my earnest expectation and my hope, that in nothing I shall be ashamed, but that with all boldness, as always, so now also Christ shall be magnified in my body, whether it be by life, or by death.

—Philippians 1:20

My prayer in the power of the Word:

_____

_____

_____

_____

_____

For I know the thoughts that I think toward you, saith the LORD, thoughts of peace, and not of evil, to give you an expected end.

—*Jeremiah 29:11*

My prayer in the power of the Word:

_____

_____

_____

_____

_____

Do It

1. Think of a blessing you recently asked God for. Examine your motivations for asking God for this particular blessing at this time. Write down your reasons for wanting it. Evaluate how well these motivations line up with the character of Christ.

2. Make a list of the ways you can be prepared for the answer you are expecting from God. Are there changes you need to make in the way you think, speak, and act? Is there anything you need to change in your physical world? Begin now to put these preparations into effect.

3. Is there anyone in your life who is negatively affecting your ability to remain positive, hopeful, and fully expectant of God's miracle? If possible, sit down and talk to that person. Gently explain the path you are on and the requests you've made of God. Invite the person to share with you her opinions or the reasons for her less-than-optimistic attitude. Express your understanding of her perspective, and ask her for help in maintaining an expectant and confident outlook.

4. Practice going about your daily tasks with a sense of expectancy. Constantly look around you for signs of God's presence and action. Expect every encounter with

another person to be God-ordained. Expect every circumstance to be divinely choreographed. Expect to be surprised around every corner. Note in your journal how this changes your demeanor and your mood. Do you find it difficult to maintain this attitude, or does it come easily? How does this attitude affect your overall feeling of contentment and peace at the end of the day?

5. Be intentional about spending time in the Word on a daily basis. Find a good Bible reading plan or Bible study, and make time each day to spend with God in Scripture. Think of this as a lifelong plan, not just a temporary fix! If you've never read your Bible cover to cover, make that your first goal. Set a realistic time range for yourself. Some people read the Bible in a year, others give themselves two or three years to get through it for the first time. Make a plan and stick to it. Ask God to reveal Himself to you through your daily contemplation of His Word.

6. Write down the ten steps in God's divine order of faith. Memorize them. Place the list where you can see it every day. Whenever you are facing a challenge in your life, approach it using these ten steps. Journal your progress, and thank God for giving you the prescription for victory in every area of your life!

Conclusion:
The Road to Your Answer

You now have the ten simple, Bible-based steps that will take you to victory over any problem you may face.

1. Identify the problem.

2. Make a quality decision to overcome the problem God's way.

3. Find your title deed to an answer in God's Word.

4. Hear the Word concerning your victory.

5. Meditate the Word to plant it in your heart.

6. Confess the Word to release your faith.

7. Act on the Word.

8. Apply the pressure of patience.

9. Wait for God's timing.

10. Expect the answer.

These steps represent God's established order for successfully operating in faith. And as we've seen over and over, divine order is a prerequisite for miracles.

You never have to experience another faith failure as long as you live. You never again have to feel the frustration of not being able to get faith to work for you as it does for others. You are now prepared to walk in the abundant, victorious life Jesus died to give you because you know how to walk in God's divine order of faith!

Notes

Chapter 3

[1]*Merriam-Webster's Collegiate Dictionary*, 10th ed., s.v. "Title deed."

Chapter 5

[1]*Merriam-Webster's Collegiate Dictionary*, 10th ed., s.v. "Meditate."
[2]*Merriam-Webster's Collegiate Dictionary*, 10th ed., s.v. "Ponder."
[3]*The NAS New Testament Greek Lexicon*, s.v. "Siyach" (by Brown, Driver, Briggs and Gesenius), http://www.biblestudytools.net/ Lexicons/Hebrew/heb.cgi?number=7878&version=kjv (accessed May 12, 2006).

Chapter 6

[1]*Oxford English Dictionary Online*, s.v. "Seven," http://www.oed .com/ (accessed May 12, 2006).

Chapter 7

[1]*The NAS New Testament Greek Lexicon*, s.v. "Ergon" (by Thayer and Smith), http://www.biblestudytools.net/Lexicons/Greek/grk .cgi?number=2041&version=nas (accessed May 12, 2006).

Chapter 8

[1]Copeland, Kenneth. *The Power Twins* (Tulsa: Harrison House, 1998).

Chapter 9

[1]*Random House Webster's Unabridged Dictionary,* 2nd ed., s.v. "Faint."

Chapter 10

[1]*Merriam-Webster's Collegiate Dictionary,* 10th ed., s.v. "Expect."

About the Author

DR. CREFLO A. DOLLAR is the founder and senior pastor of World Changers Church International (WCCI) in College Park, Georgia, and World Changers Church–New York. With twenty years of experience in ministry, Dr. Dollar is committed to bringing the good news of Jesus Christ to people all over the world, literally changing the world one person at a time.

A former educational therapist, Dr. Dollar received the vision for World Changers in 1986. He held the church's first worship service in the cafeteria of Kathleen Mitchell Elementary School in College Park with only eight people in attendance. Over the years, the ministry grew rapidly, and the congregation moved from the cafeteria to a modest-sized chapel, adding a weekly radio broadcast and four services each Sunday. On December 24, 1995, WCCI moved into its present location, the eighty-five-hundred-seat sanctuary known as the World Dome. At a cost of nearly $20 million, the World Dome was built without any bank financing. The construction of the World Dome is a testament to the miracle-working power of God and remains a model of debt-freedom that ministries all over the world emulate.

A native of College Park, Dr. Dollar received his bachelor's degree in educational therapy from West Georgia College and was awarded a doctor of divinity degree from Oral Roberts University in 1998. He is the publisher of *CHANGE,* an international quarterly lifestyle magazine with over one hundred thousand subscribers that gives Christians the tools they need to experience total life prosperity. His award-winning *Changing Your World* television broadcast reaches nearly one billion homes in practically every country in the world. A much-sought-after conference speaker and author, Dr. Dollar is known for his practical approach to the Bible and has encouraged thousands to pursue a personal relationship with God. Dr. Dollar and his wife, Taffi, have five children and live in Atlanta.

Books by Dr. Creflo A. Dollar

In the Presence of God

Live Without Fear

Not Guilty

Love, Live, and Enjoy Life

Breaking Out of Trouble

Walking in the Confidence of God in Troubled Times